WITHERN

The Story of a
Lincolnshire Parish

by

John Platt

Published by

Louth Naturalists', Antiquarian and Literary Society
The Museum, 4 Broadbank, Louth LN11 0EQ
Tel: 01507 601211
2005

Front cover:
Almhouses and Red Lion
*Reproduced by permission of Withern-with-Stain
Parish Council and the artist J M Brookes*

Printed in Great Britain by Allinson Print & Supplies,
Allinson House, Fairfield Industrial Estate, Louth, Lincolnshire, LN11 0LS. Tel: 01507 606661.

CONTENTS

Acknowledgments

Although assistance has been received from many quarters, my particular thanks go to Rex Russell for his guidance and the material he has generously provided on a number of topics. His interest led to the inclusion of aspects of village life which would otherwise have been overlooked. Lincolnshire Archives and Grimsby Reference Library staff have also been most helpful. The kind assistance of Mr Rodney Cousins, Mrs Audrey Fisk [Foresters' Heritage Trust], Mrs Anne Flower, Mr Robin Compton [Newby Hall], Mr AEB Owen, and Dr RJ Olney [Historical Manuscripts Commission] has also been greatly appreciated. My thanks to all the above and to the following, who generously provided photographs and/or documents:

Kathleen Barber	Peter McGowan
John Brookes	Doris Nicholson
Mabel Calthorpe	Edna May Newton
Frances Coote	Pam & Stewart Perkins
Margaret & Gunnar Dam	Edwin Reetham
Norman Desforges	David Sandwith
Ann & Fred Donner	Sam Stones
Pauline Forman	Morris & David Stovin
Cyril Harrison	Brian Strickland
Roy Harrison	Wally White
Alex Henshaw jr	Dr Gordon Willson
Ted Jackson	Revd Peter Yerburgh

Margaret and Gunnar Dam encouraged me to explore the Withern trail, but this book owes most to the help received from Morris Stovin and Roy Harrison [determined to see Withern's story recorded, Roy ensured that I kept going!]. I have especially fond memories of my conversations with Mrs Edna Newton [née Watson] and Mrs Annie Jackson [née Clark], which were both entertaining and helpful. Sadly, several of my 'helpers' have died while this book has been in preparation.

The Louth Naturalists', Antiquarian and Literary Society has kindly made publication possible; I am most grateful to the Society and its President, David Robinson, for the support and guidance received in its production. Thanks also to Martin Taylor for his technical help and to Allinson Print for seeing the book through the printing process. Above all, I am grateful to my wife, Tricia, for her patience and support during 'my project'.

Italics are used for quoted text; numbers in round brackets (..) relate to the 'Notes' section at the back of the book. An extensive list of the main sources is also provided. In order to cover as much as possible in the space available, style has been sacrificed in favour of content. Nevertheless, any mistakes are mine and corrections will be welcomed.

John Platt
October 2005

Introduction

"Before the first World War .. the country roads were peaceful, .. the wild flowers grew by the roadside .. and the birds sang in the hedgerows. The yellow flags - the wild iris - covered the low marshy ground by the river .. Across many fields were paths for short 'cuts' leading over the cradle bridge across the river .. Honeysuckle and the wild rose bloomed, and meadow sweet rose from the dykes giving off its scent in the night air."

[Revd George Holmes: *The Wind in the West Door*, 1968].

".. as one stands by Tickler's Mill .. the eye is carried over the meadows .. up a gentle slope .. crowned by the church of Tothill .. in the sunshine turns the great wheel of the Mill .. its waters dance in the sunlight .."

[H Green: *Town & Village Life in Lincolnshire*, c1910].

Withern with Stain [now incorporating the old parish of Tothill] is a civil parish midway between Louth and Alford. The highest point above mean sea level is 28 metres [92ft] in Tothill Wood and the lowest 2.3 metres [7.5ft] at Stain. The highest points in Withern and Stain are:-

Withern: 66ft at Woodthorpe, west of the Alford Road;
Stain: 30ft on the hill where Stain church formerly stood.

The population of Withern and Stain, 295 in 1801, is today about 450. Tothill, which had 72 residents in 1801, now has about 30.

Withern has been a settlement for over 1,300 years, yet, along with Aby, Authorpe, Claythorpe and Tothill, it is not mentioned in Arthur Mee's 'Lincolnshire'. Indeed, in Withern's case, little appears to have been written down, statistical returns are missing, parish records are few, and some known records have disappeared. Little visible evidence remains of Withern's role in mediæval times, or even during the past 250 years. It has had no resident gentry for over 200 years, has never had a 'stately home' and only briefly had a resident titled family.

For many years an 'open' parish, with more than one landowner and no resident landlord, it attracted mobile labour and was, in the 19th century, a significant centre of trade. Always a working parish, Withern was once a significant part of the de Welle estates with a large church and chantry chapel to attest its prosperity. It had a long tradition of resident clergy, unlike many neighbouring parishes, and the two resident rectors who served the parish for 40 and 30 years, respectively, from 1836 to 1907 made major contributions to the life of the community.

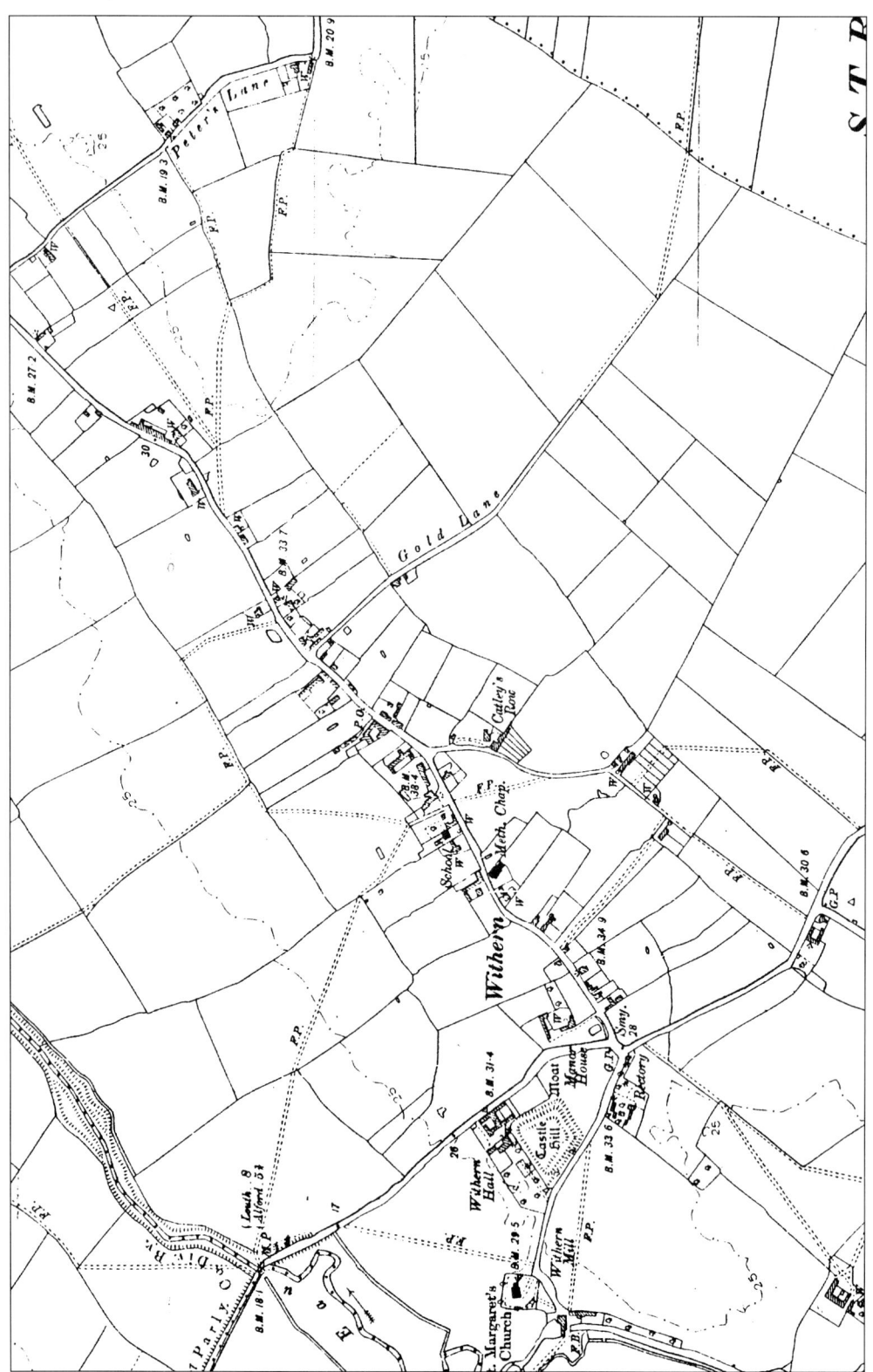

The village in the 1900s [OS map 1906].

Chapter 1

The First Thousand Years

Before the Normans

Driving through Withern today one sees little to suggest an ancient settlement. The real evidence is the name 'Withern'. Withern's roots lie in the Old English word wiðu and the Old Norse word *vithr*, both meaning 'wood'. The second element in the name is the Old English *ærn*, meaning 'house'. So, we have 'the house in the wood', probably an 8th century Saxon name, influenced by the language of the later arrivals, the Scandinavian Vikings. The name has taken many forms over the years, including Wiðerne, Wytherine and Witheren. The 'ð' was the Saxon letter *eth* - the sound 'th' in the word 'then'. Rector Glover always used 'Witherne'.

Withern is bounded on its north side by a river, the Great [or Withern] Eau. In Old English the word ea meant 'river'. In the lowlying areas of Eastern England this word eventually became 'eau', but Lincolnshire dialect still uses 'ee' or the Anglo-Saxon pronunciation 'ee-a' for the river. The original settlement, like Woodthorpe, is on the gently undulating landscape where the Wolds join the flat land of the Marsh.

British tribes in Lindsey over 2,000 years ago left barrows, marking their burials, and trackways, such as the Bluestone Heath Road. Prehistoric worked flints have been found at Stain and axeheads and a Bronze Age palstave are said to have been found in Withern. The Romans, who arrived in the 1st century AD, began to drain the marshland, the British farmers remaining alongside them. No Roman villas have been found in the Marsh, but traces of smaller settlements confirm the Romans' presence. Roman pottery has been found in Strubby and Celtic and Roman coins and Roman pottery have been found in Withern.

The Angles, Saxons and other 'German' peoples who arrived in the 6th century, extended the cultivation around the old settlements and built monasteries such as those at Bardney and Partney. 'Anglo-Saxon' pin heads and strap ends have been found at Stain.

In the 9th century the Vikings ['creekmen'] settled large areas of eastern England. The presence of different peoples is reflected in the place names - Reston and Tothill have 'Anglo-Saxon' roots, Authorpe and Strubby 'Scandinavian'. The neighbouring hamlet of Woodthorpe, called Endretorp in 1086, is another example of a place-name with Scandinavian roots. But, as populations were mixed, a 'Scandinavian' name at best only indicates that an early owner or resident may have been a Viking.

In the 6th century there was a global catastrophe of volcanic origin; the Lincolnshire coast subsided, sea levels rose and the sea inundated the coastland. The 'Anglo-Saxons' may have found the marshlands and fens desolate. The 'Danes' arrived in a wet period, but the land was subsiding more slowly. Silt from coastal erosion to the north was being deposited on the Lincolnshire shore and dunes were forming; drainage was becoming important for Withern.

The Domesday Survey

After the Norman conquest of England in 1066, William the Conqueror had a survey undertaken to establish his English landholdings and their worth. Conducted in 1086, this 'Domesday Survey' tells us that Withern had about 800 acres of arable land, 200 acres of meadow, 90 acres of woodland and a population possibly as high as 200-250; the district was relatively prosperous.

Rademer [a sub-tenant of Gilbert de Gand, the King's tenant-in-chief], controlled nearly 500 acres of arable land, with five plough teams, and had most of the meadow in the parish, a prosperous mill and the church [with a priest]. There were 20 sokemen and 13 villeins on his land.

Hugh, son of Baldric, also had land in Withern and Woodthorpe with *"underwood half a league long and as wide"*(1); and Hugh, Earl of Chester, who held land in Withern and Stain and much woodland, had six mills between Calceby and Tothill.

The Domesday Survey also names one of the earliest known inhabitants of Withern, Archil, who had witnessed Ansger extract a new toll at a Saltfleet haven in respect of 24 ships from Hastings.

The de Welles

The de Welles, descendants of Rademer, are believed to have lived at Well in the 12th century, although Robert, Rademer's great-grandson, also farmed the Honor of Haughley in Suffolk in the 1180s - the interests of the family were extending over a wide area. The first recorded presentation of a clerk to Withern Church was that of Simon made by Robert's widow, Maud, in 1220.

The de Welle family endowed local religious houses, including Louth Park Abbey [which received some woodland adjoining its grange at Aby c1150] and the monastery at Bardney, which had been refounded by Gilbert de Gand. They acquired more land and wealth through the marriage of William de Welle [d c1241] and Emma de Grainsby. Emma brought with her a hall at Aby and a close association with Greenfield priory. William and Emma, and their 13th century successors, are believed to have had a hall at Aby, but, with increasing wealth and status, they had a new mansion house built at Belleau. The de Welle family had estates in Alford, Beesby, Belleau, Claxby, Maltby, Mawthorpe, Saleby, Sloothby, Sutton, Swaby, Well and Withern - as well as land in Aby, Strubby and other places.

In 1299 Adam [d 1311] was summoned to Parliament as the first Baron de Welle. With the death of the last Gilbert de Gand without sons in 1297, he had become tenant-in-chief of the lands he held 'of the honour of Gaunt'. Adam fought in many battles for England and was Constable of Rockingham Castle and Keeper of the Forest between Stamford and Oxford (1298-1307). He built a Chapel of the Blessed Virgin Mary at Greenfield priory as the family burial place and probably built the new moated house at Belleau [described as "Clathorp, Hellou et Aby" in 1316]. Sir John de Welle, the 4th Baron, signed a document at 'Hellowe' in 1355.

Adam, the 3rd Baron, was wont to apply strong-arm tactics in dealing with those who crossed him. Court records show that, in 1339, *"Robert Sprothyng of Farlesthorpe and others .. came to Asserby and .. broke the gates of William de Asfordeby's house and entered it .. to beat William, who then fled to Authorpe [in Mumby]. [They] surrounded the messuage of Thomas de Agthorp for .. 4 days, so that William could not leave nor has he been able to go near his house in Authorpe because of the threats of Robert and Adam, lord of Well."* Again, in 1340, *"Richard de Wytheryn, servant of Adam de Well .. with others [and] .. the support of Adam .. came to the mill of 'Lothend' and .. beat, badly treated and threatened John Grayne of Covenham, reeve and miller of the abbot of Kirkstead, so that neither the abbot nor his tenants have used the mill from that day to this .."* In his will, Adam left 5 marks to 'Robert Sprotteling'; Withern's parson, Richard de Goxhill, was an executor.

The finest period for the family was the middle of the 15th century, when Lionel, or Leo, the 6th Baron [1406-61], was its head, but the family's support of the House of Lancaster led to its demise just as it reached the top of the social scale. Lionel, succeeded his grandfather, inheriting all the lands held "of the honour of Gaunt" by his ancestor Robert [d 1260]. He obtained confirmation of the weekly market in Alford [begun by William de Welle in 1283] and was knighted in 1426. Lionel was summoned to Parliament in 1432, served as Lieutenant of Ireland 1438-42, was a captain in the forces at Calais in 1451-52, and was made a Knight of the Garter in 1457. This highly promising Lancastrian was killed at the Battle of Towton in 1461 and buried at Methley, near Leeds, the home of his second wife. After his death the Well property and the barony were forfeited.

Lionel's son, Richard, the 7th Baron, survived the Towton bloodbath. Although his estates and the barony of de Welle were restored to him in 1467, he continued to intrigue against the hated House of York. He took no part personally in the Lincolnshire Rebellion of 1470, his son Robert taking command; but, when Richard and his brother-in-law, Sir Thomas Dymoke, went to London to see the king, they found that the Lincolnshire plotters' plans had been discovered. The two men were taken and executed on the orders of King Edward IV, despite a promise of safe conduct. Robert, learning of the king's treachery, joined battle with the king's army at Empingham, but his forces were totally defeated; he was executed a week later at Doncaster.(2) The family's estates were again forfeited to the king by act of parliament, although the widows of Lionel and Richard retained part as dower. Having killed off the surviving Lancastrians, the king ruled until his death in 1483.

Joan, the daughter of Richard, the 7th Baron, married Richard Hastings, a Yorkist, who was granted all the lands held by Joan's father and brother at their deaths and, in 1482, was summoned to Parliament as the 8th Baron de Welle in right of his wife.

John, the son of Lionel by his second wife, Margaret Beauchamp, lived out the last years of Edward's reign quietly.(3) Following the accession of Richard III he joined the supporters of Henry Tudor, the Earl of Richmond, in France, staying with them through to the Battle of Bosworth in 1485 and the triumph of the House of Tudor. For his loyalty to the Tudors he was married to Cecily, one of the daughters of Edward IV, and was restored as 9th Baron de Welle. The family's estates were returned to him, Joan Hastings keeping only the Willoughby estates which had come to her from her mother. John received many honours and was made a Viscount in 1486, a Knight of the Garter in 1488, joint executor to Henry VII in 1492, and a Privy Councillor in 1496. His wife's sister, Elizabeth, became the wife of Henry VII.

Viscount de Welle, Withern's last de Welle chief lord, died in 1499 and was buried in Westminster Abbey. His only daughter, Anne, died as a child. The presentation of Thomas Madiowe as Rector in 1500 by his widow Cecily was one of the last de Welle acts in Withern.

While there is little evidence today of the de Welle family, Notices of Louth [1834] records that "*in the window over the altar*" in St James' Church in Louth "*were the arms of Welles, Conisholme and Willoughby, the figure of a knight in armour; and in the bell chamber were the arms of Mablethorpe and Staynes.*"

The Mediæval Village

At the beginning of the 14th century Withern had a Norman church and a mill by the river. Close to the church, on slightly higher ground, was an earthwork, a motte created by the soil dug to make a defensive moat – probably the work of Rademer, or one of his descendants, between 1066 and 1154. It is unlikely to have been a military post and may have been a place for extracting tolls or holding a market - there was a mediæval bridge over the river where Gayton, Tothill and Withern parishes meet, recorded in 1424. However, as the de Welles never lived in Withern, the earthwork may have been designed to serve as their manorial base and an expression of the lord of Well's dominant position in Withern. It is the form of the mound, known locally as 'Castle Hill', which suggests that it was created within 100 years of the Norman Conquest. A timber structure probably stood on it, nothing having been found to suggest a stone building. Apart from the church, all the buildings in Withern would probably have been wooden, with mud walls and thatched roofs. The rectory house in Church Lane was mud and stud and probably had cottages behind it, reached by a track which ran past the rectory and down to the tofts and moated 'orchard'.

Two settlements - one by the church and one at Peter's Lane - became linked as houses sprang up along the road on the ridge, the eastern settlement being removed to make way for sheep in the 18th century. Small farms also existed near Longlands.

Most of the old field names fell out of use in the 19th century. A few mediæval names survived, such as Barfen, Beanstack Hill, Clarkes Bank, Colcroft [recorded 1338], Harlam [1186], Longlands, Ren Park, Sowfen and The Wong. Shakfen [1421] and Munchewang [13th cent] sadly did not. Names with pre-Norman roots included Asgars and Greenholm [Longlands], Hallmeer, Langmare, Marebank and Melfen.

The Land and Drainage

Before the arrival of the bubonic plague ['the Black Death' of 1349 and the 'Pestis Secunda' of 1360], when Adam de Welle held the "manor of Wytherne", the parish was a highly cultivated and prosperous agricultural area. The Lay Subsidy of 1334, a new system under which each community agreed the sum it was to pay in taxation, showed Lincolnshire to be one of the richer counties of England. The fens and the long coastal strip of marshland were the wealthiest areas in the county. Withern and Stain had a quota of £5-0s-0d, Gayton £3-0s-2d, Strubby and Woodthorpe £3-8s-2d and Tothill and South Reston £1-11s-8d. The quota for Belleau and Aby was £1-18s-0d and that for Maltby-le-Marsh £3-8s-0d.

Withern was probably mainly arable, with sheep but relatively few cattle, until the 14th century. The fens had been taken into agriculture at an early date and may well have been meadow before 1086. Monastic houses built granges [outlying farms] from which the monks drained the lowlying marsh areas. Aby was such a grange; one wonders whether Withern Grange had similar origins, being once a mansion house and farm overlooking the marsh.

Then, in the 13th century, the climate changed. In 1258 severe floods on the coast led to the establishment of Commissions of Sewers to ensure that drainage channels were cleared and banks repaired. Coastal parishes were required to maintain their defences against the sea and inland parishes to provide effective means of sending surface water to the sea - a problem in the 13th/14th centuries when storms created high dunes north of Mablethorpe. The Hagnaby chronicler records that, in 1288, "*a flood from the sea .. reached as far as Maltby field*"; St Peter's Church in Mablethorpe was destroyed and "*many men .. sheep and .. cattle*" perished. In 1315 the Louth Park Chronicle describes "*such a flood of water and rain that the fruits of the earth were entirely destroyed.*"

The authorities decided in 1345 that the cost of maintaining the sea defences should be shared by the coastal and Marsh townships, or those parts of them deemed to be in danger from the sea. Withern, with Gayton, Tothill and Strubby, had to bear its share of the burden of repairing the sea banks. Over 1,300 acres of land in Withern were charged to this work. The Withern or Great Eau, which originally entered the sea near Rimac, was diverted through Saltfleet Haven in 1347 to increase the outfall of water and prevent the port silting up. The sea's assaults on the coast were again severe in 1430 and 1499-1500.

The Church

There was probably a church by the river 1,000 years ago. When the first one was built is unknown, but, as Withern was already quite large in 1086, a church may have existed before the Conquest. Ownership of a manorial church gave status and offered advantages; the builder and his heirs not only had the right to appoint the priest, but also an interest in the tithes and offerings. The dedication to St Margaret, also used at Saleby and Well, seems to have been one favoured by the de Welles.

By the 13th century Withern had a stone church, the chancel of which was in poor condition in 1454. The neglect may have arisen from the poor quality of the mediæval clergy and the impact of the 'Black Death' of 1349-50 on the local economy. Although the Rector survived the scourge, the community at large may have been less fortunate.

The church was rebuilt in the 15th century, though little is recorded about this building. When Nicholas Madison, the Rector, died in 1607, he requested that "*my body .. be buried within my greate chancel in Wytherne,*" which suggests that St Margaret's was a large church. According to John Scargeal, the Parish Clerk in the 1830s, the pre-1811 church was large and high, with a nave 90ft long and wide side aisles.(4) The arcade in the nave had octagonal columns and well-moulded capitals. The 14th century chancel was 35ft long. At the western end of the church was a large tower with three bells in the "*steple*". Excluding the tower, the church was nearly twice the size of today's building.

A chantry altar, dedicated to St Mary, existed from 1338 until c1540. The endowment by the Rector, Richard de Goxhill, included a messuage called Chubbecroft and a toft in the east of Withern, and four acres of land in Colcroft. It provided a chalice, two ornamented vestments, two cruets, four tallies, a missal, a breviary of the Sarum use, and a chest. These probably disappeared in the 1540s at the time of the Reformation, together with other items closely associated with the old ways, such as a pair of censers [for incense], a ship [an incense vessel] and the two handbells rung at Mass.

Before the Reformation, when miracle plays were popular, Withern may have provided such theatre because Notices of Louth [1834] quotes payments made by Louth Parish Church to *"Wyderne players - vjs. viiid"* and *"for a pot of Aylle when Wyderne bayne was her - viid"*.

The mediæval church, "in good repair and kept decently" in 1602, was in poor condition 200 years later. The external walls were taken down in 1811-12 and a smaller, lower, brick shell built, integrating part of the 15th century arcade in the nave. The chancel was shortened in 1814.

Grange Farm: This aerial view of Grange Farm [centre right], taken in 1980, gives a clear view of the plan of the settlement which existed to the east of Peter's Lane until the 18th century. The fields at the bottom of the picture, below the earthworks, were an area known as Bymans Maire until the 18th century when the field boundaries there were changed. [Reproduced by permission of English Heritage. NMR]

Chapter 2:

Stain

The name 'Stain' comes from the Scandinavian steinn [stone], marking either the nature of Stain Hill or the name of a Viking settler bearing the name 'Steinn'. Stain is not mentioned by name in the Domesday Survey, but the Celts, Romans, Saxons and Danes had all been here.

In 1086 Stain was held by Hugh Lupus, Earl of Chester. The Earl's manor at Greetham, near Horncastle, had lands bordering the Great Eau between Calceby and Withern and in Mablethorpe; he also held an important manor and mill in South Ormsby. The de Stayn family, which took its name from the hamlet, held the manor of Stain under the lords of Ormsby for generations; in 1337 William de Stayn was taxed at 4s-0d in the Lay Subsidy of Edward III, the second highest level in "Wythern et Stayn". It was through the marriage of Thomas Fitzwilliam of Mablethorpe and Joan, a daughter of William de Stayn, that, after ownership by the Cumberworth and Constable families, Stain eventually passed to the Fitzwilliams.

The Church of St John the Baptist

The church, dedicated [like Belleau Church] to St John the Baptist, looked out towards the sea from the top of Stain Hill, almost as high above sea-level as the church in Withern. A spring nearby, where trees still grow, probably marks the site of the mediæval parsonage house. The graveyard lay on the Meers Bank side of the hill. When the church was built is not known, but, in 1202, the recently deceased rector had been of such a great age that no-one could say who had presented him to the living.

Richard Whyte, the rector of Stain who died in 1532, left to *the churche of Stane 25s-8d, to the payntyng off the rode loft*" and asked to "*be buryed within the churche of St John in Stane.*" He also left 10s-0d to the church of Theddlethorpe "*to the buyldyng of a steple*".

In 1548 Stain church possessed a chalice, a blue velvet vestment with thalbe, a red damask cope, a brass cross and a bell; and, as late as 1602, the church and parsonage house [a dwelling house with three bays and a little yard adjoining] were in good repair. In addition to the onset of the parsonage, there was an acre of Glebe pasture near Longlands and a meadow called Asgar's Dreane.

In 1948 a local farmer, the late 'Sam' Stones, while levelling a hillock at Stain, ploughed up a tomb containing six skeletons from the place where the church had stood. The broken 14th century stone was an incised slab, probably associated with a vault for burial within the church. The image on it is of the lower half of "*a lady in a long cote, with pointed shoes, a dog beneath her feet, its head turned to look up at her.*"(5) Little remains of the inscription and the year is missing, but the design points to a date late in the 14th century; the lady may well have been a member of the de Stayn family, possibly Joan Fitzwilliam, who died c1375.

Life in mediæval Stain was not always easy for the rector. In 1310/11 Robert de Stayn, Alan son of William, and Ralph de Roma in Theddlethorpe, were accused of having repeatedly entered the Stain rectory house and carried away corn, wool and other goods belonging to the church without permission. The three were also alleged to have repeatedly laid hands on Richard of Theddlethorpe, the rector, and to have held him in bonds. Apart from the law taking its course, they faced public sentence of excommunication in Stain church and other churches in Calcewath deanery.

The Manor House

In 1451 Sir Thomas Cumberworth, who had inherited the manor of Stain from the de Stayn family, left to "the kirk of Stayn" a brooch containing sacred relics, and to his nephew, Robert Constable, his white swans and great ball of silver bearing the arms of Stayn.

The Manor House stood on the moated site visible from the Mablethorpe road – this site is all that is left of the settlement, though farmers have ploughed up "cobbled pavements" to the west of the moat. Although Stain was only a hamlet, with two resident families in 1563, the manor house may have been grander than any house in Withern at that time.

William Talbot, who lived at Stain in the reign of Henry VIII, was a man of substance and a merchant at Calais and the only gentleman listed under 'Wytheron cum Stane' in Spring 1539 when the Muster of Calcewath was taken.

Gawen Skipwith of 'Stayne in the Marsh', who died in 1579, was the illegitimate son of Sir William Skipwith of South Ormsby and a relative of the first William Fitzwilliam in Withern. The rooms in his manor house show that he and his wife, Alice Newcomen of Saltfleetby, lived in considerable style. They comprised:
- hall
- dining parlour [with a chamber over it]
- buttery [with a chamber over it]
- little chamber
- boulting house [a room where meal and flour were prepared]
- kitchen
- milk house
- bed parlour
- crop chambers, and
- a salt house.

This household was well above the level of the 16th century yeoman farmer.(6) Outside were a hen house and a yard. The farm, leased to a tenant, had oxen, calves, cows, a bull, a few sheep, mares, a yearling horse, 2 yearling fillies, 3 foals, a nag, swine, bees and poultry. The equipment included 2 wains [wagons], 3 iron harrows, 2 ploughs, a horse mill and a grindstone. Among the crops in the fields were 12 acres of barley, 15 acres of wheat and 9 acres of beans.

At his death Skipwith's creditors included: William Fitzwilliam, Esq; John Langton of Langton, Gent; John Skipwith of Cawthorpe, Gent; Mrs Clifford of Brackenborough; and Thomas Cheifley, wheelwright.

When Francis Spendley died at Stain in 1679 his farm stock included 22 ewes, 2 tups, 14 heether hogs [males] and 10 sheether hogs [females]. A century later John Moore was shepherding sheep on Stain Hill.

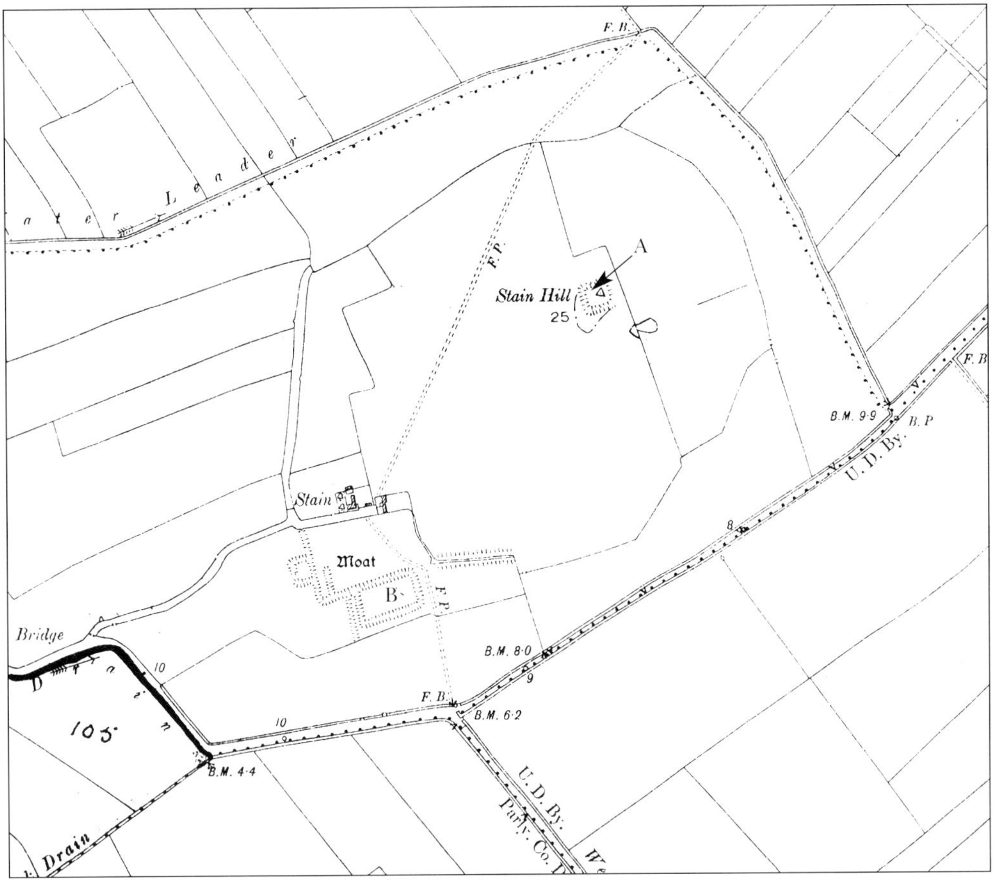

Stain, showing the sites of (A) the church and (B) the Manor House [OS map 1906].

Mr Cartwright, the ploughman, with Sam Stones and a gravestone found at the site of St John the Baptist Church, Stain, in 1948. The stone, which dates from the late 14th century, is now at Louth Museum.

William Elmhirst, who occupied the Lordship of Stain in 1765, lived at Stainsby. Stain's manor house would by then have been in decline. Sheep and pasture had become the feature of this tiny parish, remaining so until 1948 when Sam Stones, fed up with the ubiquitous rabbits, decided to plough the land for arable use and discovered the tombstone.

Stain, a small hamlet 400 years ago, remained a farm and one or two cottages down to the 20th century, located at the foot of the hill where modern farm buildings stand. The farmhouse and cottages have gone and Stain now has just one modern house, lying to the west of the old settlement.

Stain's link with Withern

For administrative purposes Stain, which covers about 250 acres, has long been part of Withern. Elmhirst made an agreement in 1765 to pay Withern's Surveyor of the Highways £1-10-0 a year to repair his road, *commonly called Stain Lane,*" and there are references in records to 'Widerna et Stein' in 1115-16 and 'Wythern et Stayn' in 1316 and 1337; for civil purposes Stain has been linked with Withern for 900 years.

The ecclesiastical parish of Stain was united with the parish of Mablethorpe St Mary in 1687 and the tithes were paid to the Rector of St Mary's from that time; a list of the Rectors of Stain is displayed in St Mary's Church. As the parish of Mablethorpe St Mary only had one church by 1705, Stain's church of St John the Baptist must have been ruinous long before the Vyners purchased their Withern estate in 1726.

```
WITHERN CHURCH OF ENGLAND
          SCHOOL
  and Guests from Leeds.



      P R O G R A M M E

            O F

      C O N C E R T.


    Friday 15th December
    Saturday 16th December
         at 2 p.m.




           FUNDS

         Comforts
 for the Lincolnshire Regiment.
```

Chapter 3:
The 16th, 17th & 18th Centuries

Building

The 16th century was a time of building in Lincolnshire. Withern's population in 1563 is unknown; Gayton's was c200-250. England's population was increasing, the price of wheat was rising, and, with land changing hands on a huge scale after the dissolution of the religious houses, the gentry were building new houses.

The Withern parsonage house may well have been rebuilt at this time. It was a mansion house of five bays in 1578 and in 1606 was described as "built with earthe & covered with thatche", three of the bays being "chambered over and boarded". In the house, the main part of which had the same ground plan as existed in the 19th century, were two parlours, a hall and a kitchen; the house and its outbuildings stood in about $1^{1}/_{2}$ acres of ground, which included an orchard and yard. The inventory of the possessions of Thomas Cooper, the Rector, who died in 1688, included:

Hall: a clock, 2 tables, 2 leather chairs, 6 wooden chairs, a mirror, etc.
Parlour: 2 leather chairs, 2 tables, 2 carpets, window curtains, etc., and a library of books.
Kitchen: a table, a dresser, wooden dishes, 2 dozen pewter plates, a dozen pewter dishes and 'other old pewter', and a still. There were also brass pots, brass pans and an iron pot.
Elsewhere: wheat, barley, malt, beans, 2 flicks of bacon.
Livestock: included 4 cows and 2 calves; 4 draught beasts, 1 steer and 3 young bulls [burlings]; 8 two-year olds and yearlings; 3 mares, 1 horse, a foal, 2 two-year olds and a yearling; 20 sheep, 14 lambs and 17 hogs [young sheep]; 4 pigs, bees and chickens.

The house had five bedrooms: two over the hall, one over the parlour, one over the kitchen, and the rector's 'best chamber'. All had bedsteads and the rector's had curtains. It was the house of a man of substance and learning.

The parsonage houses of South Reston, Strubby, Tothill and Withern were still mud and stud with thatched roofs in 1707. Authorpe Rectory was "*built of bricks and thatched with reed*" in 1724. William Jones, Vicar of Strubby 1697-1725 and Rector of Withern 1701-25, who resided in Withern Rectory, described the Strubby Vicarage House as "*built with wood & covered with straw .. [with] three rooms, the floors are clay, one of the rooms hath a Chamber over it floored with Boards,*" all in an acre of ground with "*one other Toftstead besides the Vicarage.*"

Withern Hall, the manor house of the day - and most likely the only domestic masonry structure in the parish – was probably built c1550. The only 'gentleman' in 1539 was William Talbot at Stain, but, in the 1560s and early 1570s Brian Yarburgh, gentleman, lived in Withern; an entry in the parish register records the burial in 1558 of "*Katherine, a servant to Mr Yarbrough*".(7)

Brian Yarburgh, a younger son of Charles Yarburgh of Kelstern and his 2nd wife Elizabeth Newcomen, moved to Woodthorpe after the death of his wife in 1571 and was buried at Strubby in 1579. In his will he left "*my manor house in Withern, wherein Thomas Goodwin dwells, with all the landes, .. pastures, meadows, commons .. to the same belonging*," to his son Adam, and "*one Angel of gold*" to William Fitzwilliam, whom he made "*Supervisor*" of his Will and asked "*to help my children with his counsell*".

William Fitzwilliam of Mablethorpe began to acquire lands in Withern c1578. Withern Hall, which formerly stood next to 'Castle Hill', was the "*capitall messuage*" or seat of the Fitzwilliams in the first half of the 17th century. It was still the "*Mannor house or Capitall Messuage*", known as 'The Hall', in 1664 when a deed states that it was where "*William Fitzwilliam lately dwelt*"; the Hall gate, the Milne close and the Wonge were among the adjoining closes of pasture, the Wonge being a field of 20 acres even in those days. Thomas Newcomen, the tenant for many years in the 17th century, paid £41-0-0 a year in rent for the Hall and its farmland.

Yarburgh's "*son-in-law*", Thomas Goodwin, together with William Skipwith, Edward Barker and John Lincoln, prepared the inventory of the possessions of "*Robert Barker, late of Witherne, decd.*" who died in 1611. Barker's house had a hall, parlour, chamber, kitchen chamber, kitchen, cheese chamber, buttery and milkhouse. He also had a brewing house and barn. Was he the miller? We do not know, but, intriguingly, there were boards and planks "*in the old milne howse*". His animals included 6 oxen; 6 cows; 6 yearling beasts; 5 calves; 6 mares, 2 colts and 1 filly; 47 sheep; and several pigs.

Withern Hall c1900. The 16th century manor house was demolished in the 1970s.

The Spanish Armada

After the arrival of the Spanish Armada in 1588, provision was made for the defence of the kingdom in the event of any further Spanish invasions and, in the 1590 Subsidy of Armour, the Rector of Withern, Nicholas Madison, was listed as being obliged to provide, jointly with another rector, "*a light horse*". Samuel Willingham, the non-resident Rector of Stain, was obliged to supply "*a bowe*".

Drainage

The sea continued to present dangers: St Peter's Church in Mablethorpe was overrun and "*swallowed up*" in about 1540. Thirty years later an exceptionally high tide drowned 20,000 cattle and 4,000 sheep between the Humber and the Wash. Very wet years towards the end of the 16th century caused great losses of cattle and scarcity of corn. Farmers, who now earned their livelihood mainly by cattle breeding, faced ruin; the circumstances of the labourers must have been dire.

Dykereeves, appointed by the Court of Sewers, were responsible for drainage and the sea-banks. In some cases, parishes were allowed to appoint their own dykereeves and problems arose. Although required to do so, in 1600 Carlton, Saltfleetby and Theddlethorpe failed to scour the Great Eau and floods occurred in Withern and Gayton.

In July 1664 the inhabitants of Withern, Gayton, Tothill, and Great and Little Carlton petitioned the Court of Sewers about the control of the flow of water in the river at Theddlebridge. The petition was considered before Sir Martin Lister at a meeting at Saltfleet Haven. The petitioners wanted the doors, called the Clowes, at Theddlebridge pulled up and not set down again until further order. The doors - sluice-gates controlling the flow of river and sea water in the last stretch of the Great Eau before it entered the sea at Saltfleet Haven - were felt to be too high and to create too much back water for the petitioning parishes. Many families had received "*much loss and are almost ruined by their paying rent and charges for their grounds and commonly about midsummer time when they should receive their profit they are wet with back water by the clowes long standing down ..*" The petitioners went on to demand that "*the town of Saltfletbye*" should be compelled to co-operate in the matter of the doors, so that "*we may know how high they should be and how often and how long they should take in water, that we may have our grounds no longer subject to be drowned at their pleasure ..*" The first signature on the petition was that of the Rector of Tothill, Martin Bennett. The question of doors on drains was obviously a matter of great concern, because, over 150 years later [in 1818], Robert Vyner's agent, John Burchall, objected to any staunch or door being placed across or in the Wold Grift drain leading from Strubby to the new Sea Gowt at Trusthorpe.

Sickness

Diseases were always a problem. One suffered widely in rural England was the Sweating Sickness, a devastating disease which attacked the lungs and was spread, in part, by rodents. Healthy one day, a man could be short of breath the next and dead the day after. Records begin too late to show whether the 1551 outbreak of the disease affected Withern. But, happily, the plague which struck Alford and Louth so severely in 1630-31 seems to have missed Withern and Strubby; on this occasion the country people created a temporary market outside Louth, the location still being known as the 'Saturday Pits'.

The Civil War Period

During the Civil War military action appears not to have affected Withern. In 1643 Lincolnshire was taxed heavily to support the Parliamentary Army; but, despite petitions from all over the county, only Mablethorpe, Maltby, Strubby and Withern were granted exemption "*in respect of their great loss lately sustained by the inundation of the sea.*" The three inland parishes had recently been rated at 1s-0d [one shilling] an acre for the levy for making a new bank at Mablethorpe North End; Mablethorpe was rated at 4s-0d.

In the Civil War period, apart from the Fitzwilliams, the leading occupiers of land were two sons of Nicholas Saunderson, Viscount Castleton. George [of Washingborough], who had Aby Grange, was buried at Withern in 1636. Robert, who married Bridget, daughter of Peter Christopher of Alford, farmed Grange Farm.

Early Enclosure

As late as 1664 there were still over 70 acres of woodland in the parish and much of the land around today's Withern Wood may still have been wooded. Parts of the open fields appear to have been enclosed and some arable land converted to pasture in the 1670s. Withern Wood, originally a large area, decreased in size. The furlongs in the old North Field were enclosed to form the middle fields between the river and Main Road. The western part of the South Field, a very large field which extended from The Wong, south of Church Lane, across the Aby Road and round the Woodthorpe boundary to Peters Lane, was also enclosed. Fishpond House farm [now known as Park Farm] probably came into being at this time.

When land use changed there could be a cost. In 1679 the Glebe Terrier records a payment made each Michaelmas by Aby Grange to the rectory of Withern for "*a field converted from corn to pasture about the last year of the Reign of Queen Elizabeth*" [ie 1603], according to an arrangement made then between Nicholas Madison, rector, and Nicholas Woodthorp, gentleman, the owner. This was in respect of Aby Grange land lying in Withern parish.

Harsh Times

The 18th century was not an easy time for rural families. The level of infant mortality was very high. Withern's population, c250 [50 families] in 1705, declined to c225 by 1718 [43 families and recipients of alms living in the Town's Houses], when Strubby had a population of c150 [28 families and recipients of alms].

The decline in population was probably due to the extremes of weather and widespread illness which were experienced then. A big storm on the east coast in 1696 was followed in 1703 by the 'Great Storm', one of the worst in the country's recorded experience. At Christmas 1708-09 it snowed for 12 days and there were great winds. The Christmas period of 1715-16 saw snow "*as great .. as had been known.*" In 1719, a very dry year in which little hay was made, there was a severe shortage of hands to bring in the harvest, "*agues and fevers*" spreading across the whole country in the autumn and winter. The Rectors of Trusthorpe and Manby and the Vicar of Saleby were among those who died. Agricultural labourers, unable to work or afford fuel, were again hard pressed in the winter of 1739-40 when there was a hard frost from Christmas until late February.

The Manor c1910. The manorial successor to Withern Hall built by George Fitzwilliam c1670.

Chapter 4:
Fitzwilliams & Stovins

Lord Willoughby inherits Belleau

When John, Viscount de Welle, died in 1499, William, 9th Baron Willoughby d'Eresby, received the manors of Belleau and Well, with the latter's lands in Alford; the rest of John's estates were divided between the descendants of his four half-sisters. The 12th Baron Willoughby d'Eresby was created Earl of Lindsey in 1627, but, when the Civil War ended, the family's losses led to the sale of many properties. Sir Henry Vane bought the Earl's Belleau estate in 1651 and demolished the church of Swaby St Margaret. After the execution of Sir Henry Vane, the estate was re-granted to the Earl of Lindsey by the restored Charles II. Although the parishioners of Aby had kept their church decently and well repaired for many years in the 17th century, it was not long before a survey reported the chancel to be in some decay *"through the fault of the Lord Willoughby of Earesby proprietor of the parsonage"*. The survey also reported the church and chancel at Well to be "ruinated" for the same reason. The heritors of the de Welles were no longer seriously interested in the area. Little evidence remains of the priory at Greenfield, where, according to White's Directory for 1826, *"the moat is still entire, but of the building nothing remains but the foundation."*

The Fitzwilliams acquire Withern

One of Viscount de Welle's half-sisters, Margaret, married Sir Thomas Dymoke. Her descendant, Robert Dymoke, sold his one-fourth part of the manor of Withern in 1578, *"along with a messuage and appurtenances in this vill and Malberthorpe"*, to William Fitzwilliam, who purchased another portion from Arthur Hall of Grantham in 1579. Hall later sold Woodthorpe to John Ballett.(8)

At his death Maurice Berkeley, grandson of Catherine de Welle, possessed *"half the manor of Witherne held of the Earl of Surrey of the Manor of Louth .."* In 1583, when Elizabeth, the sister and heir of John Berkeley, died, she held one-ninth of the manor of Withern and one-ninth of the advowson.

The blood link in Withern's ownership, which had existed from the 11th century, continued. William's father, a descendant of Margaret de Welle, was George Fitzwilliam of Mablethorpe, the son of John of Skidbrooke who had inherited the manor of Mablethorpe and Stain in 1536 [Lincolnshire Pedigrees describes the Fitzwilliam arms as - 'lozengy argent and gules, in fesse a fleur-de-lis of the second within a border sable bezanted' - being a mixture of the Fitzwilliam and Mablethorpe families' arms]. In 1597 William was the first Fitzwilliam to be buried at Withern. His son Robert, of Mablethorpe, was buried at Withern in 1601; another son, Sir George Fitzwilliam [who sold the Mablethorpe estate in 1613], was buried at Withern in 1637.

When the Herald's Visitation of 1634 listed the Gentry of Lincolnshire, the only name under Withern was Thomas Newcomen, the lessee of Withern Hall for

Gravestone of George Fitzwilliam [1664-1704].

These stones were formerly located in Withern Church. The gravestone of George Fitzwilliam can no longer be seen and the Lister Fitzwilliam memorial has been destroyed. The Stovin stones are now in private hands, although Richard Stovin's memorial is broken.

Memorial to Lister Fitzwilliam [1700-68] and his first wife, Mary Stovin [1699-1749]. [Reproduced by permission of English Heritage. NMR]

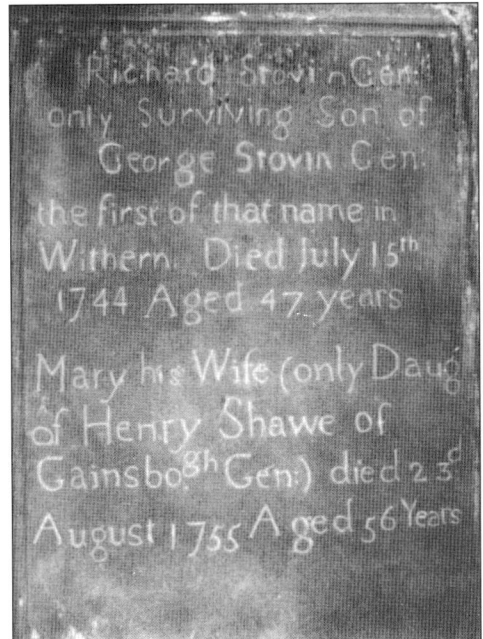

Gravestone of Richard Stovin [1697-1744] and his wife, Mary Shawe [1699-1755].

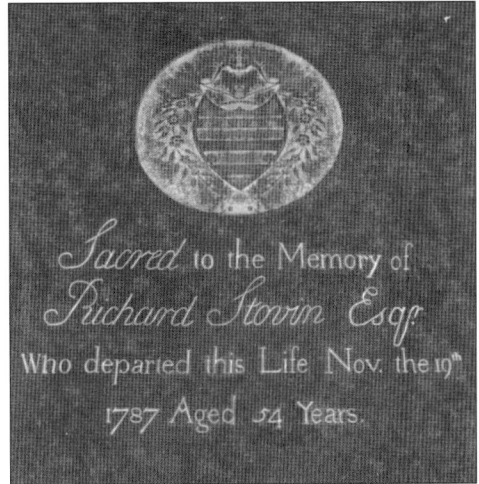

Memorial to Richard Stovin [1733-87], containing his crest. The Stovin family crest is described in Fairbairn's Crests of the Families of Gt Britain & Ireland as 'a bow, in fess gules, transfixed by an arrow, erect and flighted, of the same, headed, argent'.

many years before 1686 whose daughter Sarah married Charles Ballett of the Woodthorpe family].

At this time William Fitzwilliam [1610-78] was living in a "*mansion house*" in Louth, where he was Warden in 1670 and 1677. When he married his first wife, Elizabeth Cresswell, in 1632 it was "*reported to Archbishop Laud that Mr. Fitzwilliam had made a clandestine marriage with Mistress Creswel, being married by a fire-side instead of 'in facie ecclesiae'.*" Their son George [1636-82] boosted the family's fortunes by marrying Martha, daughter of William Lister of Coleby, near Lincoln. Three children were baptized in Lincoln before George and Martha moved to their newly built Manor House in Withern in about 1673.

Arrival of the Stovins

George Stovin [1664-1729], "the first of that name in Withern" according to his tombstone, came from Crowle c1695 and married a Withern girl, Elizabeth Stocks. The Stovins were early Dissenters, Baptist or Quaker, and George's grandfather [a leader of the Epworth Riots in 1651] had been imprisoned in Lincoln Castle, where he is said to have died in 1656/57. George moved to Withern with his brother Cornelius [d 1726]. Although Dissenters, George and Cornelius were friends of the Revd William Jones [Vicar of Strubby from 1697 and Rector of Withern from 1701]; he entered the births of their children in the parish register as 'Anabaptist', as Anglican baptism had not been used. George's son and daughter only began attending Church services in 1715 and several more years elapsed before they agreed to be baptized.

Cornelius II, son of Cornelius, moved to Gayton. At the start of the 19th century his descendants were in Great Carlton, where their gravestones can still be seen. The 'Cornelius' branch continued the family's non-conformist tradition and, with the purchase of Aby Grange by Cornelius Denison Stovin in 1898, restored the family's association with Withern.

The Stovin Estate

It is not clear when George Stovin made his first purchase of property in Withern, but it seems to have been Grange Farm. The first transaction of which a record has been found was in 1697 when Stovin, "*of Wytherne*" and a mercer or merchant in the wool trade, bought a farm in Peters Lane from Charles Fitzwilliam [1654-99], the lawyer half-brother of George Fitzwilliam, the builder of The Manor. This sale had been forced on Fitzwilliam by John Ayre of Louth in the terms of a financial agreement made in 1693. In 1709 Stovin acquired Corner Farm from Thomas Newcomen. By 1723 he had retired to Saltfleet Haven.

An interesting footnote on the postal system of the day is a letter, dated 8 December 1756, from Henry Shawe, in Wakefield, to George Stovin II, addressed to "*Mr Stovin at Withern near Alford, Lincolnshire*" and marked "*Turn at Stilton. Single Sheet only.*" One can imagine the horse rider coming down the Great North Road, supping at an inn in Stilton and then turning off in an easterly direction into the remote parts of Lincolnshire!

The Last Fitzwilliams

The Fitzwilliams were constantly short of money, so much so that, in 1686/87, William Lister, Martha's brother, made agreements with his nephew, George

Fitzwilliam [1665-1704], under which Lister took title to various properties to ensure that the Fitzwilliams found the money needed to pay the portions due to the younger children under their father's will. George was then a grazier, who provided grazing for the cattle of other landowners, such as George Langton of Langton Hall, who, in 1690, paid George Fitzwilliam 6d a week for two three-year old steers and 4d a week for three steers and two two-year old heifers.

When George died the shackled estate passed to his brother William [1673-1724], who left it to his surviving son Lister. Lister sold the major part of it to Robert Vyner of Gautby in 1726 to pay the family's debts, losing the lordship of the manor, the patronage of the Church, and Withern Hall, but retaining two properties - the Manor House and Laurels - and over 325 acres of land. The Revd John Marriott, who arrived in October 1726 wrote in the parish register that the entries for 1725 "*were writ by Mr Lister Fitzwilliam during the sequestration.*"

A descendant of Rademer and of Walter de Gand, Geoffrey Plantagenet, William de Grainsby, Elizabeth de Mablethorpe, Joan de Stayne, the lords Deincourt, Greystoke and Mowbray, the Dymokes of Scrivelsby, the Skipwiths of South Ormsby and the Listers of Coleby, Lister was baptized at Withern on 6 March 1700. His first wife, Mary, the daughter of George Stovin and Elizabeth Stocks, died in 1749. In 1751, at Authorpe, Lister married Susanna Stocks, the daughter of John Stocks of Withern. Both marriages were childless.

The Stovins helped Lister financially and, in his will, he left his estate in Withern to his first wife's nephew, George Stovin, with a life interest to his [Lister's] widow Susanna. When he died in 1768 Lister was buried in the chancel of Withern Church by the Revd John Marriott. His sister Sarah, who had married Samuel Lindsey, died in 1778, aged 81, and was buried in Withern. Susanna, Lister's widow, farmed in Withern until 1797, when she released her remaining 210 acres to Richard Henry Stovin in return for an annuity of £100 a year. When she died in 1802, her bequests reflected the genteel life formerly enjoyed by the Fitzwilliam family.

The families of George [d1704] and William [d1724] Fitzwilliam were buried at Withern for over 100 years, the last being Grantham Hodgson of Louth [1773-1858], a descendant of George's daughter Martha. Grantham Hodgson was lord of the manor of Maltby-le-Marsh in 1842 and, as late as 1882, a Colonel Moore was Maltby's lord of the manor "*in right of his wife*", Hodgson's grand-daughter.

The Stovin Estate Rescued

It is ironic that both the Fitzwilliam and Stovin estates in Withern should have become bankrupt. When Richard Henry Stovin [1774-1818] inherited in 1787 his family's estate was in good order. However, while his father had been content to be a gentleman in Louth, young Richard, an army officer, chose to live beyond his means. In 1810 he was resident in "*York Street, Portman Square, Middlesex*", leaving his estate in the care of Thomas Mountain, who lived at Grange Farm. In 1817 Mrs Stovin died in "Curzon Street, London"; Richard died in Bath in 1818, aged 43.

Before he died Richard had run out of money. Happily, his nephew and heir, Richard Stovin Maw [1786-1862], with the support of the mortgagors and some essential, but minor, sales, retained the insolvent estate. Thanks to his management - and, for over 30 years, the able assistance of his agent and kinsman, Joseph Coulam [1771-1851] - it existed for another 100 years.

Chapter 5:
The Vyners

Who were the Vyners, lords of the manor of Withern for almost 200 years?

Robert Vyner [1631-88] left Eathorpe, the Vyner family's Warwickshire estate, and went to London, where he became the leading goldsmith of his day, a baronet in 1666 and Lord Mayor of London in 1675. He spent £30,000 on remaking the regalia for the coronation of Charles II in 1661 and advanced large sums to the king during the Plague and for the wages of the Army and Navy. Neither the king nor Parliament felt inclined to repay the £416,000 he lent the king in 1677 [the IOU can be seen on a staircase wall at Newby Hall in Yorkshire]!

Sir Robert acquired an estate at Tupholme in Lincolnshire. He had two older brothers - Samuel [ancestor of the Vyner rectors of Authorpe and Withern], who inherited the family estate at Eathorpe, and Thomas, Dean of Gloucester, whose son Thomas inherited Tupholme [his descendants were mostly called Robert!]

The 1st Robert [1683-1777], who was MP for Grimsby and later Lincolnshire, built Gautby Hall, near Horncastle, one of the 'lost' great houses of Lincolnshire. Among the large areas of land he acquired were the manors of Withern [1726] and Authorpe [1750] and the lease of Strubby rectory [1754].

The 2nd Robert [1717-99], MP for Okehampton 1754-61, Lincoln 1774-84 and Thirsk 1785-96, married Eleanor, daughter of Robert Carter of Redbourne, Lincolnshire, and was step-father to the 1st Lord Yarborough.(9)

The Lady Theodosia Mary, daughter of the Earl of Ashburnham and wife of the 3rd Robert [1762-1810], gave Gautby Hall a period of glittering social activity. But their son, the 4th Robert [1789-1872], High Sheriff of Lincolnshire in 1814, was a bachelor and preferred to live in London. Gautby's condition deteriorated. When The Lady Mary Gertrude Robinson married Robert's brother Henry she was given Newby Hall, near Ripon, by her father, Earl de Grey.(10) The next generation preferred to live at Newby. Gautby Hall, no longer required, was demolished in 1874.

The estates passed from the 4th Robert to Henry and Lady Mary's unmarried eldest son, Henry Frederick Clare Vyner [1836-83] and from him to his brother, Robert Charles de Grey Vyner [1842-1915], a humorous, sociable man, and an aficionado of the turf. After a few years in the Grenadier Guards, he devoted himself to his 26,700 acres, sport [especially his horses], his chateau on the French Riviera and Newby Hall. He was widely travelled, adding to his fascinating collection of chamber pots as he went round the world; the collection is on display at Newby Hall.

The 5th Robert's daughter, The Lady Mary Evelyn, who married a son of the Marquess of Northampton, disposed of her Lincolnshire estates after the Great War, the last 1,120 acres in Withern, Authorpe, Mablethorpe and Stain being sold in February 1920. Her final act in Withern was to present the Revd RP Norwood as Rector in September 1922, her patronage of the Church being transferred later to the Bishop of Lincoln. Lady Mary, the last Vyner 'chief lord', died in 1957, aged 91, and was buried alongside her father, mother and husband in Skelton-cum-Newby churchyard.

Robert Vyner [1717-1799].
[Reproduced by permission of the Earl of Yarborough]

The Revd Dr Robert Vyner [1753-1804], Rector of
Authorpe. [Reproduced by permission of the Earl of
Yarborough]

Robert Charles de Grey Vyner [1842-1915].
[Reproduced by permission of Mr Robin Compton, Newby
Hall]

Colonel H W Vyner [b. 1821], brother of Revd W P Vyner
and author of 'The History of the Vyner Family'. [Reproduced
by permission of the Shakespeare Birthplace Trust]

27

Chapter 6:
Withern Mill

The mill recorded in the Domesday Survey probably stood at the same point on the river as the present buildings. Upstream, Claythorpe and Tothill also had mills, the river being a focus of industry as well as a source of food - it was once noted for its trout and grayling. Today the river has been 'improved' and agriculture has changed. Only the mill building, with its water race beneath, now stands. The mill is likely to have been the undershot type with a mill leet to produce a satisfactory head of water on a slow-moving river. Certainly, the Tickler family had such a mill in the 19th century.

Watermills existed from the 8th century or earlier and the Withern mill may have existed before the Conquest. It was worth 15 shillings a year in 1086, being quite a valuable property for its locality. The owner was Gilbert de Gand and Rademer, his man-on-the-spot, was responsible for the manorial mill, where all tenants would have had their corn ground.

When, in 1115, Walter de Gand raised the priory at Bardney, refounded and endowed by his father Gilbert, to the rank of a free abbey, he added more endowments, including $2^{1}/_{2}$ bovates of land in Strubby, a bovate in Woodthorpe and the mill at Withern. At the dispersal of monastic lands in Henry VIII's reign the possessions of Bardney were granted to Sir Robert Tyrwhitt. From the year 1115 the Mill was never in the ownership of Withern's main landowners.

The Newcomens

When Ralph Cooke, the miller, died in 1652 the inventory of his estate showed him to have been a man of substance. The lease of the mill and its grounds was valued at £80-0-0 and the whole inventory at £130-1s-8d. Thomas Newcomen, Thomas Craford, Ambrose Etherington and Robert Keale signed the inventory of Ralph's estate, which portrayed a typical household of the time:

Hall:	a counter table, two chairs, a dishboard, two forms and a woollen wheel.
Great Parlour:	a trandle bed, bedding and a cupboard.
Little Parlour:	a bedstead, a feather bed and covering, a pair of blankets, a pair of sheets and a chest containing linen and other household goods.
Dairy:	two butter firkins, cheeses, shelves and milk vessels; two sooes, two brass barrels, a kitt and a churn.
Outside:	a foal and two fillies, two cows, a calf and four pigs; four loads of hay, straw and old wood were also listed.
In the Mill:	four sacks and five barrels of malted corn, together with a millstone, two ganelocks and other items.

Withern mill and mill house c1910. The waterwheel is visible on the left below the mill building.

By the mill pool c1910.

The Newcomens owned the mill; in a deed of 1717 Thomas Newcomen referred to his "Grist Mill .. known [as] Wythern Water Mill" with its oatmeal kiln and house. Thomas Gunnil was the miller in 1709, John Manby in 1766 and another John Manby in 1780. When Catherine Newcomen, of The Close, Lincoln, died in 1793 [she is buried in Lincoln Cathedral], she left her Withern property to Catherine Lawrence, who sold it in 1795/6.

The Arrival of the Ticklers

A 'Mr Gilbey' appears to have been the miller in 1795, but William Tickler had arrived by the summer of 1796. When Tickler died in 1834, the Mill House he had built and the "Corn Water Mill" passed to his son George [1789-1836]. George, who ran the mill for some years before his father's death, added a "Wind Corn Mill" [a postmill], which stood for over 40 years. He was listed as a 'miller and baker' in an 1835 directory, when he owned a "*brick and tiled dwelling house*" and a "*baker's shop and oven*" adjoining the old Methodist Chapel. After George's premature death his widow, Jane, ran the business with their young sons, Isaac and William, and the boys' half-brother George Riggall Tickler [1811-81]. William died in 1855 [he left £50 to Eliza Ann Fawn, who was the governess to Annie Grant at Withern Hall], but the mill was already being run by his half-brother, George, who had married Jane Marshall, sister of the Red Lion publican.

One of those who gained his early experience of milling at Withern Mill was Thomas Willson. His father was innkeeper of the Kings Head in Alford and his sister married the miller and baker at what later became known as the Station Mill. Thomas no doubt learned many of the basics of milling there, but, by the early 1830s he was working at Withern, where he lived with the Ticklers. Following his marriage he settled as a miller in Huttoft where he built the Alford Road mill.

According to John Saunderson, the Louth millwright, the postmill erected in the 1830s, which stood in the mill yard beside the dam, collapsed while corn was being hoisted into the mill. One of the spurns [quarter bars] gave way and the mill fell into the dam; one of the Tickler sons, working inside the mill, escaped. Saunderson later pulled the windshaft out of the dam. This event may have prompted installation of a turbine to drive the water mill, because the business had "*steam and water mills*" from 1881 until the Great War. However, by 1881 changes were taking place in milling. Flour from windmills and watermills, using locally grown wheat, was slowly being superseded by flour from larger mills, which used imported hard wheat. Smaller mills eventually gave up the business.

Milling was not without its hazards for the Tickler family. One morning in 1881 George Tickler, 70 years old and "*a man of energy*", was trying to set the waterwheel in motion from the outside when he lost his balance, fell between the wheel and the breastwork, and was crushed as the wheel began to turn. His wife and two employees dragged him out and over the board and carried him into the house in an armchair. When Dr Hurley arrived George was in bed upstairs. Some ribs were broken, but the doctor suspected internal haemorrhages, as George was breathing with difficulty. Another doctor said the case was 'hopeless'. William Jarvis spent the afternoon reminiscing with George about their 55 years in Withern until George died at 6.00pm. The Inquest verdict was accidental death, the Coroner stressing that George had put himself in danger.

The mill was the village bakery throughout the 19th century. George Tickler was miller, baker and corn merchant, his son Fred [1857-1909] adding 'flour and offal dealer' to the list. Daily deliveries of plain bread, seed bread and plum bread were made to the village shops before the Great War; during the war the Supply Stores opened its own bakery behind the shop to supply the village.

The End of the Mill

George's widow, Jane [who went to live near the new Methodist Chapel when Fred married in the 1890s], died in 1904, aged 82. After Fred's death in 1909 the Ticklers formed a company, Withern Fishing and Estates Ltd, to own their lands in Withern and the mill was leased for a few years to Joseph Hoyles, a well-known miller and baker in Maltby-le-Marsh.

Withern Fishing and Estates Ltd sold the mill in 1919 to Harry Wright, a local farmer, whose daughter, Grace, remembered the mill much as it would have been in the Tickler's time. In the 1990s she could still recapture "the lovely smell of freshly baked bread as it was turned out of the tins". Her father delivered the grindings to the farmers in the district by horse and cart; the bread he took around the neighbouring villages in big baskets, the children riding with him. Progress, in the form of a lorry for delivering the goods, eventually led to Phoebe, the gentle horse, being pensioned off.

The mill house of the 1920s had five bedrooms, two front rooms and a very large kitchen and pantry, with cupboards and a big cooking range. It had a bathroom and a water toilet [there were also several outside - three in the garden and two in the back yard near the Brew House!]. A hand pump was used to fill the water tank for domestic use [which involved 100 pumps each for the children]. In a nearby field an automatic water-raising machine, known as a ram, sent water about half a mile through a pipe into a pond at Withern Hall farm, where the Scargills then lived.

The house had an attractive garden, along the boundary with the churchyard, divided into four small gardens by box hedges; and there were orchards where the children played. In 1994 one of the big yew trees was still standing and an old chestnut tree, in full bloom; a bay leaf bush still grew beside the place where the Wright family's pets were buried. While the four small gardens were now just one large expanse of grass, the orchard was still producing apples and Victoria plums. Playing near a river had its dangers then as now; Grace remembered George Marwood, a village boy, falling in and being saved by one of her brothers.

In 1926 Charles Berry, then owner of Withern Hall, acquired the mill, which continued in operation for a few more years with, first, Mrs King as the miller and, finally, Mrs Marion Smith. The mill was closed in 1936 and, in 1938, it was bought by the Surrey Trout Farm. Over 850 years as a watermill had come to an end. The mill house was demolished in 1964.

Tickler's Jam

The Tickler family's main claim to fame came as the producers of Ticklers' Jam. Thomas George Tickler [1852-1938], Fred's older brother, who was educated at Louth Grammar School, became an engineering apprentice in Hull. In 1877 he moved to Grimsby, becoming a corn factor and grocer. It is said he began to make jam at home, using fruit from the orchards at Withern Mill; it is true that around 1880 he began manufacturing jam and acquired a flour mill in Grimsby, where he installed three boiling pans. 'TG', who married Walliss Thomas Wells' daughter Fanny Louise, later opened a factory in Pasture Street and became Mayor of Grimsby in 1907 and MP for Grimsby in 1914. His company flourished during the Great War, its plum and apple jam being used throughout the Services. The word 'Tickler' became a widely used Services term for cigarettes, the jam and cigarette tins being of similar size. Soldiers also adopted the name for 'Tickler's Artillery' - firing the empty jam tins, filled with nails and metal objects, at the enemy! The Tickler family has always remembered its links with Withern.(11)

Chapter 7:
Farming 1750-1920

Farms in the 18th century

In 'English Society in the Eighteenth Century' Roy Porter saw England in 1700 as *"still a second-rate rustic nation of hamlets and villages .. Nearly eighty per cent of the population lived in the countryside, and almost ninety per cent were employed either in agriculture or in processing rural produce."*

The impact of harsh weather and disease on such communities can be imagined. While the severe frost in the winter of 1739-40 hit the labourers hard, the farmers, too, suffered when cattle plague spread across the whole country in 1747, large numbers of cattle being lost in Lincolnshire.

Who were the farmers? In 1754 the main tenants of the Vyner Estate in Withern, and their yearly rents, were:

Stephen Frow	£90-0s-0d
Thomas Showler	£76-0s-0d
John Badley	£65-0s-0d
John Dinsdale	£53-0s-0d
William Showler	£42-0s-0d
William Dales	£12-0s-0d
Michael Porter	£9-16s-0d
Wm Betteson	£9-0s-0d
Joseph Kerman	£8-16s-0d
John Blakey	£8-10s-0d

Tenants paying rentals below £8-0s-0d a year were:

Thomas Lancaster
John Harrison
James Vere
James Drury
John Johnson
Christopher Harrison
James Dunham
Mary Dover
The Revd Mr Marriott
Vincent Cotton
and John Greswell.

The rents receivable from the estate amounted to £422-16s-0d.

Other Withern farmers in 1754 would have included Lister Fitzwilliam [The Manor], George Stovin [Grange Farm], and Samuel Lindsey, Lister Fitzwilliam's brother-in-law [Laurels].

Lincolnshire } A Dublicate or Assessment for
Lindsey } raising an Aid to his Majesty by a
Land Tax of Four Shillings p Pound upon all Lands in
the Parish of Withern with Stain for the Year 1795.

Proprietors	Rentals £ s	Occupiers	Sum Assessed £ s d
	50. 0	John Holland	10.. 0.. 0
	45. 0	Tho.s Showler	9.. 0.. 0
	1.. 0	John Clark	0.. 4.. 0
	4.. 0	Jos.t Storey	0 ..16.. 0
	4.. 0	Nic.s Simpson	0 ..16.. 0
	2. 10	Wid.w Dales	0 ..10.. 0
	43.. 0	James Enderby	8.. 12.. 0
	5.. 0	John Spence	1.. 0
	8. 10	W.m Dales	1 ..14.. 0
	4.. 0	W.m Bontgt	0 ..16.. 0
	8.. 0	Geor.g Wear	1.. 12.. 0
	7.. 0	John Blakey	1.. 8.. 0
Rob.t Vyner Esq.r	6.. 0	Tho.s Lanchester	1.. 4.. 0
	4.. 0	W.m Johnson	0.. 16.. 0
	23.. 0	John Dinsdale	4.. 12.. 0
	6.. 10	Wid.w Hewson	1.. 6.. 0
	22.. 0	John Holland	4.. 8.. 0
	7.. 0	James Porter	1.. 8.. 0
	34.. 0	Benj.n Grant	6.. 16.. 0
	7.. 10	Peter Bullivant	1.. 10.. 0
	1.. 0	W.m Cotton	0.. 4.. 0
	81.. 0	Tho.s Mountain	16.. 4.. 0
	26. 10	John Walmsley	5.. 6.. 0
	5.. 0	W.m Bullivant	1.. 0.. 0
Rd. Hen.n Stovin Esq.r	13.. 10	Tho.s Borman	2.. 4.. 0
	2.. 0	Dan.l Finch	0 ..8.. 0
	14.. 0	John Upton	2.. 16.. 0
M.rs Fitzw.m	32.. 0	W.m Fitzwilliams	6.. 0.. 0
	4.. 0	Semper Stocks	0.. 16.. 0
	20.. 0	W.m Griffin	4.. 0.. 0
Willoughby Wood Esq.r	30.. 0	John Thompson	6.. 0.. 0
Alford School Land	11.. 0	Rob.t Lucas	2.. 4.. 0
Rev.d M.r Mowncey	55.. 0	Tithe and Gleabe	11.. 0.. 0
Langton Esq.r	3.. 0	Tho.s White	0.. 12.. 0
M.r Brereton	21.. 10	George Bellamy	4.. 6.. 0
	16.. 0	M.r Gilby	3.. 4.. 0
M.rs Lawrence	2.. 0	Wid.w Manby	0.. 8.. 0
	2.. 0	John Bullivant	0.. 8.. 0
Rob.t Vyner Esq.r	107.. 0	M.r W.m Elmhirst	21.. 0.. 0
	6.. 0	D.o for Stain Gleabe	1.. 4.. 0
		Total £	140.. 17.. 4

Benj.n Grant } Assessors & Collectors
John Upton }

28.th May 1795

Allowed by Us.

Tho.s Wayet

Fr. Ji Wills

Henry Colston

In Strubby the 'Strubby Rectory', comprising "*the Rectory and Parsonage of Strubby .. and .. all their Grange called Strubby Grange ..*" including all lands, Glebe Lands and the "Vicarage or Mansion House used by or for the Vicar there," had been leased from the Church by Robert Vyner. The farm now known as Manor Farm, but then called the Glebe Farm, was let to John Lill, who paid £100-0-0 a year in rent in 1754. Lill died shortly afterwards and his widow later married Samuel Desforges, who was the tenant in 1771.(12) By the 1830s Joseph Wilson was there; his grand-daughter married Willows Farrow and was the mother of the well-known Victorian cattle breeder Joseph Wilson Farrow.

By 1780 changes had occurred, Withern's main farmers being:

> William Cotton [Grange Farm]
> John Badley
> William Bentley [Withern Hall]
> Thomas Showler [Park Farm]
> John Upton
> John Keal ['Village' Farm]
> Benjamin Grant [Sindy]
> John Walmsley
> William Holland
> and Robert Griffin [Laurels].

John Elsey was farming at Aby Grange and George Bellamy at Woodthorpe. John Upton and Robert Lucas were the Assessors and Collectors for the Land Tax.

Many of the farmers, such as the Stocks, Desforges and Showler families, were related and Robert Griffin was married to Ann Stocks, Susanna Fitzwilliam's sister.

1800-1850: A Time of Many Changes

Greater change occurred at the end of the 18th century. By 1809 the main farms and their tenants were:

> Grange Farm [Thomas Mountain]
> Withern Hall [John Holland]
> Manor Farm [Matthew Sandon]
> Park Farm [John Desforges]
> Longlands [William Jacklin]
> 'Village' Farm [James Enderby].

Medium-sized farms were:

> Sindy [John Young]
> Brook Farm [Thomas Wells]
> Laurels [William Griffin]
> Corner Farm [Philip Willows].

Aby Grange was now farmed by John Robinson.

These were not easy years; farms changed hands often. William Cotcheifer followed John Holland at Withern Hall and Richard Grant took over Manor Farm. In 1816 Joseph Coulam followed Thomas Mountain at Grange Farm. The 1832 Land Tax Assessment contained several new names, among them William Loughton, Thomas Marshall, John Mawer and Samuel Robinson; William Cotcheifer and William Gresswell were the assessors.

The Napoleonic Wars were the topic of the day. In 1798 Withern, like most parishes, collected money "*for the Defence of the Country*", raising £69-11-0. After

Name	£	s	d	Name	£	s	d
Appleyard Mrs	7	5		Holland Jno	121	2	6
Bullivant Mrs	3	10		Johnson Wm	4	5	
Bullivant Peter	9	10		Julian Mrs	16	0	
Do	8	10		Kelk Geo.	1	5	
Bullivant Thos	8	10		Lucas Robt	15	6	
Suckling Mr	55	16		Lancaster Thos	6	5	
Dent of Wm	6	5		Mountain Mrs	150	0	
Bellamy Mr	16	0		Do a Cottage	6	5	
Maud Thos	3	5		Porter James	9	16	
Cotton Wm	2	0		Robinson Mr	50	2	6
Dales Mrs	3	3		Loughton Mr	10	0	
Dales Wm	12	0		Story Mr	4	0	
Wells Mr	35	17	6	Barker Mr	6	4	
Desforges Jno	70	0	0	Simpson Nichs	5	0	
Enderby James	55	0	0	Sandon Mr	90	0	
Finch Danl	1	0		Tickler Mr	26	0	
Griffin Wm	30	0		Vear Geo.	9	0	
Gresswell Mr	5	0		Wright Mr	5	0	
Young Jno	49	10		Killows Mr	28	10	
	388	1	6		564	1	0
					388	1	6
					952	2	6

Rentals Chargeable to the Church Assessment for 1809. [Reproduced by permission of Sussex Archaeological Society/Lincolnshire Archives]

Robert Vyner, who gave £50-0-0, the main donors were Mrs Fitzwilliam [£5-0-0], the Rector [£3-0-0], John Holland [£1-1-0], the Curate [£1-0-0] and Mrs Elizabeth Dales, John Dinsdale, James Enderby, Benjamin Grant and James Porter, who each gave 10s-6d. No Stovin tenants appear to have contributed. Strubby raised £2-3-0, Samuel Desforges giving £1-1-0 and Thomas Wells 10s-6d.

There was another change in the last decade of the 18th century. The Stamford Mercury carried a Notice in July 1796 that "*the principal inhabitants of Withern .. taking into Consideration the many evils and Inconveniences attending Annual Feasts, and being well persuaded that the Abolition of them in this Parish will prevent many irregularities .. resolved .. to DISCONTINUE that Custom*". This action was said to arise from the Feasts falling "*in harvest*" – usually on the first Sunday in August – but may have had as much to do with the company the Feasts attracted, such as pickpockets and prostitutes. Interestingly, the Curate, the Churchwarden, Mrs Fitzwilliam, John Holland, Thomas Mountain and William Tickler were among the 17 signatories, but some farmers, such as Benjamin Grant, John Dinsdale and Thomas Showler, were not.

A very bad harvest in 1799, "*the year of the dearth*", was followed by several poor ones and the price of wheat rose, making life hard for labouring people. By 1810 commerce was in crisis and bankruptcies were commonplace. RH Stovin was steeped in mortgages and his estate lacked investment. When Richard Stovin Maw inherited it he spent "*nearly £2,000*" on drainage, "*before which low land was at times flooded*". The drainage work coincided with the building of the Trusthorpe 'Sea Gowt and Race' in 1819-20, which was heavily influenced by Robert Vyner.

For years the weather was unpredictable, but, happily, the Vyners, although absentee landlords, showed concern in bad times. In the severe winter of 1820-21 Robert Vyner provided 160 men's slops [or carters' frocks], 50 bed rugs and 220 men's and women's neck handkerchiefs for the poor on his estates in Withern, Strubby, Authorpe and Claythorpe.

In 1826 the summer was so hot and dry that the rivers and canals in Lincolnshire almost dried up, the marshes and fens were parched, and cattle and sheep died due to lack of moisture. The Stamford Mercury reported "*three deplorable years*" [1826-28] being followed by a wet, cold and windy harvest in 1829 - the "*most unpleasant one since 1799*". Despite better farming methods, farmers were having a difficult time. John Desforges, who bought Corner Farm from the Stovin Estate in 1821, went bankrupt, his attempt to become a landowner, rather than a tenant, being foiled by the mortgage he had and the harsh years he experienced. Labourers' wages were low and poor families faced long winters.

Accidents and dishonesty did not help. George Coulam was badly wounded by one of William Harrison's cows in 1842, just as he was due to take over Longlands. And Charles Ward, who worked for John Mawer of Aby Grange, was convicted at Lindsey Quarter Sessions in Spilsby in 1840 of embezzling various sums of money from his master. He was sentenced to three months hard labour and "*to be once privately whipped.*"

The improving Lincoln Red shorthorn cattle and Lincoln sheep [bred from New Leicester rams and Old Lincoln ewes] played an increasingly important part in the mixed farming of the area [the Coulams bred Lincoln Reds], but, in the 1830s and 1840s, there were still farmers who were constantly in arrears with their rents. Not all tenants appreciated it, but efficiency was becoming essential for survival. In 1846 one of Maw's tenants was heavily in arrears with his rent because his way of farming was poor: *"for years [he] has had too much corn & far too little green."*

Maw, who visited his estate regularly, took a close interest in everything, as his programme in June 1850 illustrates. Arriving by train at Claythorpe, he was met by Joseph and George Coulam and taken to Withern in a dray. After a supper of fowl and ham he went to bed at 11pm. An early riser, he was up, writing, at 5am before setting off in the dray with Coulam senior to visit Longlands, Mablethorpe, Maltby, etc, during the morning. After dinner he rode around the fields east of Grange Farm with George before going to Manor Farm. From there he walked back to Grange Farm, calling on the Loughtons at Laurels, William Jarvis at Gold Lane, and John Tyson at Fairview. The following day, after receiving their rents, he walked with each tenant over his land. After tea at Manor Farm he had a *"prozy chat"* with the Rector, much of it about George Stovin's charitable bequest of 1729.

Life was getting better. Improvements continued, the value of the Stovin lands being enhanced by four times the cost of the tiles after the drainage work undertaken in 1850. The labour force was in balance with the number of jobs available; wages, although not generous, were reasonable.

Enclosure

Following the Enclosure Act of 1836, the landowners sought to enclose the remaining common fields. No longer would farmers have strips and sections in common fields co-ordinated by Field Reeves appointed annually in open meeting. Withern's farmers appear to have wanted enclosure - certainly the Stovin tenants did. The landowners convened a public meeting in 1838 to discuss the matter and, on 30 July, the required number consented in writing to enclosure. Two Commissioners were appointed and a plan of the open fields made by the Surveyor. Before making any division of lands, the Commissioners set out the public carriage roads and highways through the open fields and scoured, widened and deepened the old ditches, drains, gates, bridges, etc. The area to be enclosed was 589 acres and 29 perches, and 7 acres, 3 roods, 10 perches were allotted for the public and private roads. The Commissioners held a public meeting at the *"house of Thomas Marshall known by the sign of the Red Lion"* on 26 November 1840 where the Award was announced; it was signed on 7 January 1841.

The main allocations of land were to Robert Vyner, Richard Stovin Maw, John Ballott Fletcher of Woodthorpe, the Revd Dr John Parkinson [owner of Corner Farm], the Revd WP Vyner [Rector] and the Governors of Alford Grammar School; lesser amounts were allocated to Maddison Orry, Dr John Calvert and four others [the Parish Clerk received half an acre - 'Rogue's Acre'].

Enclosure had little impact on rents, as the following table illustrates:

Farm	Year	Tenant	Acres	Rent /year	Rent /acre
Grange Farm	1814	T Mountain	372A-1R-02P	£500	£1.34
	1821	J Coulam	333A-0R-33P	£500	£1.50
	1840	J Coulam	331A-3R-38P	£506	£1.52
	1852	G Coulam	269A-2R-38P	£415	£1.54

Longlands	1814	R Garniss	122A-0R-17P	£180	£1.47
	1821	J Jackson	120A-1R-32P	£196	£1.63
	1840	J Coulam	124A-2R-22P	£201	£1.61
	1852	JC Drewery	151A-2R-36P	£244	£1.61
Manor Farm	1814	R Grant	179A-3R-36P	£264	£1.46
	1821	R Grant	193A-3R-33P	£280	£1.44
	1840	W Grant	197A-3R-17P	£318	£1.60
	1852	J Parker	213A-3R-01P	£337	£1.57

[*Grange Farm, the Stovin estate's "best farm by far" in 1851, had the lowest rent because the tenant acted as Agent for the estate; Maw stayed with the Coulams on his visits to Withern].

The public roads appointed were:

- the 'Louth and Alford road', 30 feet wide, from the parish boundary at Woodthorpe Hall to the end of the field where the culvert passes under the Alford road;
- the 'Strubby road', 30 feet wide, from Carrott's Corner to the Strubby parish boundary;
- the 'Stain road', 30 feet wide, from Calfen lane to Barfen lane and through the open field near 'Longlands Cottage'.

The following private carriage roads were also appointed:

- the 'South Field occupation road', 25 feet wide, extending southwards from Gold lane;
- the 'East Field occupation road', extending northwest from Stain road [ie the Barfen lane].

After enclosure of the East Field, Barfen Farm was created by the Vyners and run as a satellite of Withern Hall. Maw built Enderby's Yard [Longlands Cottage] to serve the lands in that area associated with Manor Farm. 'The Glebe', an area of 30 acres on Stain Lane opposite Grange Farm, had a crew-yard and barn, which were removed by Sauls after World War II.

Enclosure introduced the rectangular fields, bounded by hedges and dykes, which once were seen between Withern and Woodthorpe and between Stain Lane and the river. Many fields have since been merged. Some trees and hedges which have disappeared in recent years - for farming reasons or due to disease – may have dated from 1840.

1850-1875: Larger Farms and Agitation for Better Wages

An impression of the number of jobs available on farms in Withern and Tothill can be gained from the following table, which shows the size, the number of workers employed from outside the immediate family, and the number of female servants recorded in the 1851 Census at the main farms:

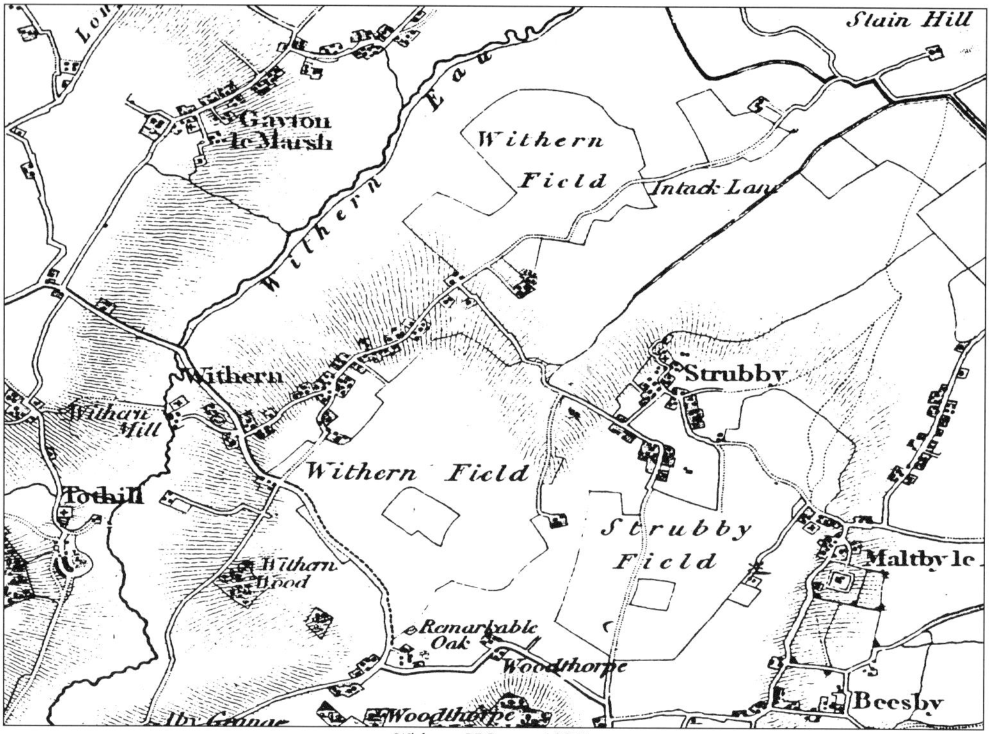

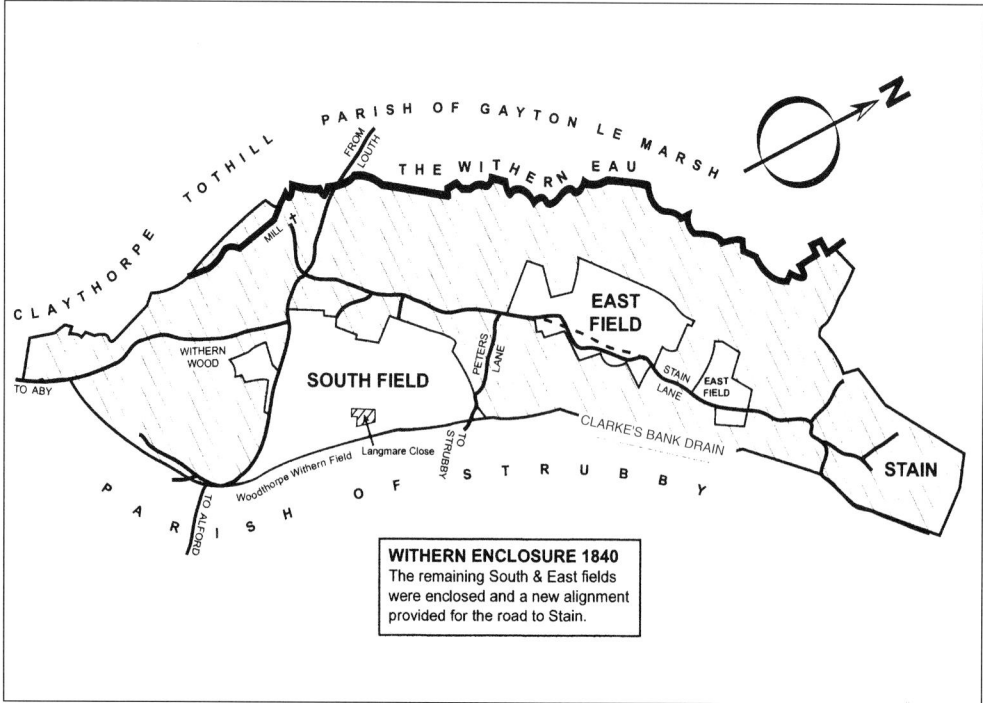

Withern [OS map 1824]

WITHERN ENCLOSURE 1840
The remaining South & East fields
were enclosed and a new alignment
provided for the road to Stain.

The South and East Common Fields enclosed in 1840. Langmare Close in the South Field was an enclosed area belonging to the Stovin estate.

Farm	Farmer	Acres	Labourers/Farm Servants
Withern Hall	William Grant	606	30 outdoor, 2 indoor, 2 females
Grange Farm	George Coulam	321	12 outdr, 6 indr, 2 boys, 3 females
Park Farm	Thos Robinson	230	3 outdoor, 2 indoor, 1 female
'Village' Farm	Edward Barker	220	7 outdoor, 2 indoor, 2 females
Manor Farm	Joseph Coulam	197	7 labs, 2 boys, 2 females
Brook Farm	John Wells	160	5 labs, 1 female
Longlands	J C Drewery	135	4 labs, 2 females
Sindy	James Enderby	98	10 outdoor, 2 indoor, 1 female
Laurels	James Loughton	83	4 outdoor, 3 indoor
School Farm	Geo. Hutchings	60	1 lab
Vear's Farm	George Vear	49	1 lab, 1 female
Red Lion Farm	Thomas Marshall	46	1 man, 1 boy, 2 females
Willows	Richard Atkin	45	
Home Farm	John Kirman	31	
Fairview	John Tyson	20	1 female

Tothill

Farm	Farmer	Acres	Labourers/Farm Servants
Tothill Manor	William Barker	295	4 outdoor labs, 3 indoor
Glebe Farm	Benjamin Spore	60	2 indoor labs, 1 female
Cooks' Farm	John Cook	47	2 indoor labs
Shaws' Farm	Joseph Shaw	21	

In 1851 there were shepherds at Grange Farm, Brook Farm, Stain and Woodthorpe, over 100 Withern men and 11 Tothill men finding work on farms. Today the number of full-time workers employed on farms is about half a dozen.

Joseph Coulam, after 35 years with the Stovin family, died in 1851. Following his death the Stovin farms were "*altered and arranged*"; Grange Farm was reduced in size and Manor Farm, Longlands and the Gold Lane farm were enlarged.

In the decade 1860-70 the Vyner estate also re-organized some farms. When Edward Barker, grandson of the Revd William Sisson, died in 1866 his large farm in the centre of the village [called, for the purposes of this volume, 'Village Farm'] was added to Thomas Marshall's to create the 20th century's Red Lion Farm. When George Vear died in 1860 and James Enderby jr in 1870 their lands were re-distributed among the larger farms. The Vear farmhouse was removed and Sindy's thatched farmhouse became cottages.

Withern's labourers were not as badly exploited as some. The Vyner Estate appears to have been a good landlord, although there was no 'great house' and no 'estate' housing, such as is found around Brocklesby. Maw built houses nearer to their places of work for some of his labourers in the 1850s - an improvement as advantageous to him as to them.

When the 1867 Parliamentary Reform Act failed to give the farm workers a vote, they felt aggrieved and became receptive to trade unionism. Early in 1872 the Eastern Morning News reported that "*awakening of the agricultural labourers [was] proceeding with astonishing rapidity*". In Withern "*a meeting of upwards of 200 labourers took place in Mr Lusby's booth .. and it was resolved to agitate for a general advance of 6d per day in wages. It was also determined to form a labourers' society.*"

In April the Stamford Mercury reported that "*a crowded and enthusiastic meeting of labourers was held at Lusby's inn, Withern .. The idea of a strike was entirely repudiated, the object of the society being to send abroad those whom the farmer could not afford to pay fairly ..*"

1875-1914: Agricultural Depression

The prosperous years of farming and the labourers' agitations ended by 1875, when the Agricultural Depression began - a difficult period which lasted until the Great War. A combination of bad weather [reducing crops] and imports of cheap wheat from North America [reducing prices] ruined many farmers. Alternative sources of income were explored. John Mawer of Aby Grange built a flax mill, to which Flaxmill Cottages bear witness. But, the number of jobs on farms declined and labourers moved to the towns; some emigrated.

The Three Tuns ["Lusby's booth"] closed c1876, a casualty of the population change and, probably of its association with the agricultural workers' agitations. Pauline Gregg in her 'Social and Economic History of Britain' observed that: "*The farmers, the magistrates, the clergy, the publicans – all whose concern it was to keep agricultural wages low, labourers servile, and their pennies directed to the beer-house instead of the union – continued their subversive day-to-day work.*" Henry Vyner and his agent probably found an opportunity to close the pub, leaving the labourers no option but to use the Red Lion, where the recently widowed Mrs Marshall and her son John Tom would keep an eye on them [the Marshalls farmed 220 acres and employed 5 men and 2 boys on the farm and a man to brew the beer]. The Red Lion alone now served Withern's refreshment needs.

Foot-and-mouth disease and rinderpest were serious problems in the 19th century. In 1883 nearly half a million animals were affected and it was said that most crew-yards in the Marsh, from Spilsby to the sea, had a little wicken cross set up as a counter-spell against witchcraft. For "*Mr Wells of Withern*", who had about 400 sheep at Partney Sheep Fair in 1882, "*prime lots, which realized from 50s to 54s*", disease on this scale must have been very worrying. Outbreaks of foot-and-mouth continued and became so bad that the cattle, sheep and pig sections of the Royal Agricultural Society's Show at Doncaster in 1912 were cancelled.

Poor harvests and a stagnating economy from 1875 led to a decline in trades union membership by 1878. Prices for wheat were at their lowest in 1893-95 and the Depression at its worst in 1894-95. As in the early years of the 19th century, the difficulties were made worse by the extremes of the weather - 1904 and 1914 were too dry; 1903 was very wet. In the worst year, 1912, there was little sunshine, warm spells in early summer, and an exceptionally violent storm at Lincoln in mid-June, giving an inch of rain in twenty minutes. After one of the coldest and wettest Augusts on record, there were two days of violent gales and, in November, a week of severe frost with heavy falls of snow.

Weather predicting, a valuable talent in the countryside, was not always given credence. Billy Loughton, who farmed Laurels, was walking back from Calf Fen one fine afternoon when he passed Amos Bullivant, who lived at Hillcrest. Billy warned Amos that a storm was coming and advised him to secure his stacks and loose items. Amos laughed. Not long afterwards an almighty storm arose, much damage being done - and Amos Bullivant suffered his share. Little damage occurred at Laurels! The Loughtons left Withern before the Great War, taking their rustic skills to Canada.

Longlands c1918.

These cottages on Main Road were once the farmhouse of Benjamin Grant and James Enderby jr; they are today the house known as 'Sindy'. Photographed in 1950 by MW Barley. [Reproduced by permission of Mrs D Barley/English Heritage. NMR]

After the Great War

    The increasing taxation introduced in the 1900s led to many old estates being broken up and sold after the Great War at a time when land prices were high. The Edwardian days of high society had gone. The boom period for agriculture during the Great War ended with the removal of Government support in 1921. The economic depression in the 1930s was a difficult time for farmers; although the Government introduced subsidies on various farm products and restrictions and duties on imported foodstuffs, farming did not return to its former prosperity. The revival in agriculture came with the increase in support and production during World War II.

Sale of the Old Estates

    When he died in 1862 Richard Stovin Maw, who lived at Staines in Middlesex, left the Withern estate, still subject to a mortgage of £13,000, dated 21 July 1820, in trust to his two daughters. One of the daughters, Harriett, married William Anthony Mitchison, wealthy grandson of a London silk manufacturer. The estate, which had passed to Richard Stovin Maw in 1818 and been left virtually intact by him to his daughters in 1862 [only Corner Farm and the close called 'Coal Croft' had been sold], was sold by the Mitchisons in 1918/19, The Manor being described as the best house in the estate and The Grange as the second best [any close links the family had with Withern had effectively ceased when Joseph Coulam's son George died in 1872].

    The last properties of the Vyner Estate, including Withern Hall, were sold in lots at auction in 1920 by Lady Mary Compton-Vyner; several had previously been sold privately.

Axemen including Henry Watson, Fred and Henry Dennis, Tothill Wood c. 1914

Chapter 8:
The Churches

The Church of England

From 1600 to 1900 Withern had 14 rectors, 11 of whom resided in the Rectory. Probably 8 rectors and 2 curates were buried in the church or churchyard. In only about 25 years, chiefly in the 18th century, was there no resident clergyman; in Authorpe, Strubby and Tothill incumbents were often non-resident and curates lacking. Withern's church was well provided for, being in the top 20% of valuations in the district. The following table compares the values of some local livings [KB is the King's Book]:

Eccles. Parish	Annual Value 1535 [KB]	1856	Pop. 1851	Patron 1856
Authorpe	£ 5-13-4	£166	126	Robert Vyner
Gayton-le-Marsh	£13-10-0	£500	326	Ld Willoughby de Broke
Stain	£ 5-06-1		-	-	-
Strubby with Woodthorpe	£ 4-13-4	£150	287	Dean and Chapter of Lincoln
Tothill	£ 6-17-0	£137	59	Ld Willoughby de Broke
Withern	£18-10-2½	£500	503	Robert Vyner

The rebuilding of St Margaret's Church in 1811-12, wherein were displayed the Commandments, the Creed and the Lord's Prayer, reflected the plain Protestant religion of a century earlier, when William Jones *"read Publick Service on Holy Days, and .. once every Lord's day"* - Jones had not held services on every holy day because he had *"no congregation, this consisting wholly of working people."* By the end of the 18th century the parish was finding the repair and upkeep of the old church beyond its means - *"a very ancient building .. become so ruinous and decayed .."* (13) The building of the new church, which does not appear to have been assisted by the Vyners, received little architectural input. One report says nothing from the old church's ritualistic past was retained - *"not a vestige of old furniture was left, not a moulded beam, bench end, or even a scrap of old stained glass."* The musical instruments from the previous century were sold. The three bells from the old church tower were also sold - to pay for new seats - and a small bellcote was put up containing a single bell. The cost of rebuilding was met by a rate on the parish and the proceeds of the sale of materials from the old church. The chancel was retained, but the rector had it shortened in 1814.

The century following the Fitzwilliams' loss of the lordship of the manor was dominated by two rectors - John Marriott and John Mounsey. Marriott, the first rector presented by a Vyner, was a dealer in property and a man with firm views on everything - many of which he entered in the parish register. When Aaron Andrews became parish clerk in 1758 he was said to be "*no singer! but a good Reader.*" Descriptions of parishioners included: "*a notable whore*", "*a notorious strumpet*", "*young but pious!*", "*an old crabbed cottager*" and, of an old farmer, "*an helpless man, came to no church! a poor dish*". Among the events at which he officiated were the baptisms of the brothers George Stovin [1727] and Richard Stovin [1733], the marriage of Sarah Fitzwilliam and Samuel Lindsey [1734], and the burial of Lister Fitzwilliam [1768]. It was Marriott who covered the front of the mud and stud rectory house with the red brick seen today.

John Mounsey, Rector from 1789 and a man of "*pecuniary means, rank in society, [and] kind disposition*" according to the Vicar of Minting, lived at Gautby, visiting his parishioners in Withern and Authorpe "*twice every year*"! William Sisson, his 'Officiating Minister', looked after the parishes and co-operated with the Methodists; they ran a joint Sunday School in 1816.(14) Sisson appears to have been a very conscientious minister in the plain Protestant tradition. His daughter Jane married a local farmer, William Barker, at Gayton in 1820. Her son, Edward Sisson Barker, farmed the 'Village Farm' in Withern c1843-66. A younger son, William, farmed at Tothill Manor.

Although Mounsey was an absentee rector, he provided a resident 'officiating minister' throughout his incumbency. At first Sisson lived at Authorpe, being also curate for Dr Vyner, the absentee Rector of Authorpe. But, the old, thatched Authorpe Rectory was no longer suitable and he moved to Withern c1794. According to Mounsey, Withern Rectory was "*rebuilt by .. Dr Vyner*" in the 1790s, no doubt to provide his curate with a decent home.

When Sisson died in 1823 he was succeeded as curate by his son, William Lowther Sisson [later Sisson-Wayet], who had been born in Authorpe. Mounsey had hoped that a Vyner would be found to take on some of his responsibilities, but these hopes were dashed by the early death of John Vyner, a member of the Gautby family who appears to have been destined for the Church.

In part, the arrival of William Phillips Vyner, as Rector of Withern and Authorpe in February 1836, fulfilled Mounsey's hope. Vyner began his duties on Sunday 26 June. Failing to find lodgings in the parish of Withern, he found accommodation in a farmhouse in Gayton. In late September he told the Bishop he hoped "*to be resident in the parsonage house at Withern*" in a fortnight, "*but the late curate of the parish has not yet left it*"! Poor Sisson Wayet; after spending 15 years taking care of the spiritual needs of Withern he had been given notice to quit.

When he finally gained access, Vyner, nephew of Dr Vyner and an aristocratic bachelor, renovated the Rectory and rebuilt the outbuildings; he also created the garden familiar to many older Withern residents.(15) The local clergy in the 1840s were, socially, a group apart. William Layng, newly arrived as curate in Strubby, described them thus: "*Being the only resident gentlemen in the country, [they] employ themselves entirely in their gardens .. The villages here are so very thinly populated & yet [there are] so many Baptists (who are most bigoted against the Church & will not even receive clergymen into their houses) that [there] is but very little weekly duty in most parishes about.*" John Allett, the Rector of Maltby-le-Marsh, helped his less skilled clerical colleagues to brew their own beer. While suspecting that his Midlands reader would think that he was surrounded by "*a queer lot of people*", Layng gave as his own conclusion that "*the clergy here do everything for one another, [and] are not nearly so high & lofty*" as many he had

St Margaret's Church as it looked c1930.

An external view of the east end of the church in 1978 [the church had closed in 1973]. [Reproduced by permission of English Heritage. NMR]

47

The 15th century font, which now stands in the burial ground [photographed in the church in 1978]. [Reproduced by permission of English Heritage. NMR]

A stone sculpture, preserved from the mediæval church, on the wall beside the main door; it disappeared after the church was sold [photographed in 1978]. [Reproduced by permission of English Heritage. NMR]

View of the chancel in St Margaret's Church c1965. The east window donated by TG Tickler depicted St Margaret, St George and the Ascension.

48

been accustomed to. William Vyner asked Layng if he was fond of retirement and country amusements, because "*the clergy in this neighbourhood wd not exist if they cd not garden & do their own carpentering*." Carpentry was Vyner's hobby - he incorporated a carpenter's shop in his rebuilding of the Rectory.

Churchgoing in Withern and the surrounding parishes was the custom of about half the population in 1851; it appears to have been most popular in Gayton and least popular in Strubby and Tothill. However, as Rector, Vyner was also chairman of Withern's Parish Vestry, enabling him to exercise benevolent control over parish affairs. He was a quietly generous man and, in 1848, shared with the 4th Robert Vyner the cost of rebuilding Authorpe Church. His relationship with his Gautby kinsman was good and, in his will, Robert Vyner left him a legacy of £1,000 and an annuity of £200 for life. Having been Rector for over 40 years, William Vyner retired to Louth, where he died in 1878; he was buried in Louth Cemetery.

Frederick Glover, who arrived in 1877, a man of distinction, with degrees in arts, law and music, was one of the most popular rectors the parish ever had. He was described by one writer as "*a musical parson .. [whose] musical abilities have .. proved of immense value in attracting worshippers to his services, and considering the smallness of the parish, the congregations which assemble at Witherne Church on Sundays are phenomenally large*." During his 30 years in Withern he formed a church choir and a village band made up of agricultural workers. He taught the band members their notes

Interior of the church showing the vaulting which survived from the mediæval church [photographed in 1978]. [Reproduced by permission of English Heritage. NMR]

and instructed them how to play, the band becoming one of the most competent in the district. Glover, who was a JP and for a time Diocesan Inspector of Schools for the Lincoln Diocese, was a most popular rector who made a great contribution to village life. He chaired Parish Council meetings, by invitation, for 13 years.

Noel Swayne succeeded Glover in 1907. Another active rector, who showed concern for his parish in a patriarchal way, he enlarged the Rectory in 1911 to house his young and growing family. After war service as an Army chaplain, he left Withern in 1919.

Methodists

The first Methodist gathering in the district appears to have been in Tothill in 1791, but in 1796 the newly-arrived William Tickler began holding Methodist services in his house in Withern.

The Methodists' success led them to seek proper accommodation and, early in December 1809, they registered with the Bishop of Lincoln a "*newly erected*" non-conforming chapel in the parish. A noted Methodist preacher from Mumby, George Robinson, preached in Withern in December 1809, possibly at the opening service in the chapel on Main Road. Built on land owned by William Tickler [and now part of 'The Haven'], it was described in 1849 as "*a chapel with a small graveyard*" - in which some early Methodists, notably Ticklers and Loughtons, were buried. Other early Withern Methodists included Thomas White [the carpenter] and the Bontoft, Cumberworth, Hoff and Hutton families. William Barker, the shoemaker, was Steward when the Religious Census was taken in 1851; Census Sunday congregations numbered 120 [morning] and 140 [evening], with 30 Sunday Scholars at each session.

When the population of Withern was at its peak, the old chapel was too small to cope. William Askey agreed to provide a site for a new chapel on his land across the road, taking the old chapel in exchange for use as a warehouse.

The Memorial Stones of the "*New Wesleyan Chapel & School-Room*" were laid on 19 October 1874 by Mrs Joseph Bryant, Mrs George Riggall, Mrs M Lill, Mrs S Grant, Miss ME Riggall and LH Bryant. The Revd RW Starr of Hull gave an address at the site and preached in the old chapel in the evening. "*A Public Tea*" was provided at 5 o'clock, "*Tickets One Shilling each*". The collection amounted to £83-3s-2d. The Trustees of the new chapel were:

Joshua Bryant	G Atkinson	John R Young	R Riggall
A Riggall	WG Riggall	S Grant	John Mawer
W Sutton	Thomas Carter	W Loughton	R Loughton
RW Orry	R Addison		

An Alford architect, Mr A Wood, designed the chapel and the contractors were Carters of Withern. Mr Rowe of Strubby did the brickwork. The slates came from a Welsh slate quarry. Some of the original slates, dated 1874, have calculations etched on them [for the slate cutters' work] and the names William Parry, Owen Thomas and Thomas Thomas.

The chapel and adjoining schoolroom [which cost about £800, raised by public subscription] opened for worship on 28 June 1875. A harmonium and heating were added later. The sittings ['pew rents'] were let for the first time on 9 July 1875,

To the Right Reverend Father in God George Lord Bishop of Lincoln.

We whose Names are subscribed do hereby certify that the Dwelling House in the Occupation of William Tickler situate in the Parish of Withern in the County and Diocese of Lincoln is intended to be used as a place of Religious Worship for those of His Majesty's Protestant Subjects dissenting from the Church of England commonly called Methodists And we do request that the same may be registred in your Lordship's Registry according to the act of Parliament in that Case made and provided Dated the 8th. Day of September in the Year of our Lord 1796.

William Tickler
John. Adlard
Wm West
John Goe
Jam Co_
Wm Barton

The application for the registration of William Tickler's house in Withern as a place of religious worship by the Methodists, 1796. [Reproduced by permission of Lincolnshire Archives]

the cost being one shilling a seat for six months. Memorable names of regular worshippers in the 1870s were:

Allett, Askey, Atkin, Badley, Beels, Blanshard, Carrott, Carter, Clark, Coney, Coupland, Drewery, Evinson, Fenwick, Fussey, Harrison, Keal, Larder, Loughton, Maidens, Marshall, Marwood, Mountain, Orry, Patchet, Ridall, Searby, Sivel, Skelton, Tickler, Tyson, Vear, Watson, Webster, White and Wilson,

representing a cross-section of society - farmers, shopkeepers, craftsmen and labourers.

Primitive Methodists
In 1813 the Withern house of Elizabeth Dales was licensed for use "*by an Assembly .. of Protestants*". It is not stated whether this was a breakaway group of Methodists or a Baptist congregation. There was a Primitive Methodist congregation in Withern, but this came later. A group of 'Protestants', led by Edward Orry, owner of the Village Stores, applied in 1841 for a certificate to allow them to use "a warehouse", occupied by Orry, as a place of religious worship. The 1851 Religious Census says a Primitive Methodist congregation worshipped in a Main Road "*dwelling house*" which had been "*built before 1800*". It was probably one of the buildings behind the shop in Orry's Yard [now Gledhill Drive]. Edward Orry was the Steward and the average attendance was 17.

'Dissenters'
When William Vyner arrived as Rector the life of the community was changing. While the Church may still have had the power and the support of the landowners, the Chapel was attracting increasing support from the people. Vyner, who, in his brother's words, "*led a retired life*", was well respected, but must have found the changing world hard to accept. He appears to have had little time for 'dissenters'.

Withern Mill in the 1930s

Chapter 9:
Schools

Early Schools

The Church provided education until the 18th century – but only for a fortunate few. A grammar school associated with the church at Strubby in 1264 continued into the 14th century. In 1663 the Strubby Glebe Terrier refers to "*one barne & part of the yard whith some hay*" being "*given towards the maintenance of a schoole*". A few were educated by priests; Thomas Gonville, son of a Rector of Authorpe and himself Rector of Tothill in 1659, was educated at "*Horncastle, Withern and Lynn*" before going up to Caius College, Cambridge. His teacher in Withern may have been John Walker, the Withern Rector.

The 18th Century

The first recorded school in Withern was held in the Church in 1718, Francis Johnson teaching English and grammar and catechizing 30 scholars from Withern and neighbouring parishes. To be a teacher, Johnson had confirmed that he adhered to the faith of the Church of England, as defined in the 39 Articles, and that he did not believe in Transubstantiation, and had agreed that he would conform to the Liturgy of the Church of England.

William Jones, the Rector who arranged this schooling, valued education. When he died in 1725 he left £50 to pay for teaching children of the poor of Withern parish. The land in which this money was invested is still owned by the William Jones Foundation, a registered charity, which distributes its income annually in Withern. When George Stovin died in 1729 he left £100 to be used for teaching poor children. The two bequests helped to provide schooling in Withern for many years.

The Early Years of the 19th Century

In about 1800 Robert Vyner provided a building on Main Road in which the Church ran a school; 16 children attended, free of charge, for "*instruction .. in English reading and the Church Catechism*." The schoolmaster was paid from the Jones bequest and private donations. This small school only touched the surface of the need, the curate, William Sisson, observing in 1818 that the poor in the parish were "*without sufficient means of educating their children*." Some would probably have attended the Sunday School run jointly by the Church and the Chapel.

This Church School [master Samuel Parrish; mistress Miss Lucy Gawthorpe] had 23 boys and 7 girls in 1835, 15 paid for from charitable sources, the rest by their parents. By 1841 William Elger had succeeded Parrish as schoolmaster.

Two other schools in Withern, opened in 1833, had 1 boy and 14 girls paid for by their parents; one was a boarding school run by a Revd Thomas Dainty. A Methodist Sunday School gave free instruction to 42 boys and 27 girls. As late as 1871 Jemima Horsewood, in Peters Lane, ran a 'Dames School'.

A New School

In 1850, to meet the growing population [and no doubt under pressure from the Rector], Robert Vyner provided the land for a new school and a School House, the National Society contributing £35-0-0 towards the cost of the new buildings.(16) Withern now had a purpose-built National School, costing £350-0-0, and a qualified schoolmaster, Thomas Knight, from Gravesend, who received £32-0-0 a year and a rent-free house. Lucy Gawthorpe, who remained as schoolmistress until c1855, received £20-0-0 a year.

The school was extended in 1858, enabling the 'schools' to provide an area of *"six feet to a child"* [in those days boys and girls were housed separately]. A Government grant of £148-10s-0d was received. Two schoolrooms, 48ft x 15ft and 32ft x 15ft, were deemed capable of accommodating 100 children without inconvenience. Average attendance in 1858 was 65 [38 boys and 27 girls].

Sunday schools also played an important part in education, 51 children [28 boys and 23 girls] attending the Church Sunday School in 1858 and about 40 the Methodist Sunday School. By 1861 Church Sunday School attendance had risen to 104.

The Vyners and the School

The National School was not wealthy; it relied greatly on the generosity of the Vyners. In 1851 the School's income was £62-0-0, of which £41-0-0 [66%] came from the Vyners, the Rector himself finding £31-0-0 [50%] from his own pocket - he still provided about £30-0-0 a year in 1858 and maintained a small Dame's school for little children in Authorpe, the older Authorpe children attending the schools in Aby, South Reston and Withern.

After paying the salaries of two teachers, the rest of Withern School's income was spent on books, coal, etc. In 1872 the school was supported by a Government grant, the Jones and Stovin charities, private subscriptions and the scholars' weekly pence. Private donations included £10-0-0 a year from Edmund Vyner, the Rector's brother, and, from 1874, £12-0-0 a year from William Vyner, who was now in his late sixties; even in retirement he paid £6-6-0 a year.

School Attendance in the 1860s

In 1861 Withern's population [528] reached its highest recorded level. 140 children were on the school's books and 111 attended regularly. Thomas Knight was still the schoolmaster and Harriet Woods, who lodged with the Withern postmistress [Rebecca Desforges], was the schoolmistress.

William Vyner told the Royal Commission on the Employment of Children, Young Persons and Women in Agriculture in 1867 that *"if children go out to work in the fields they must work all the day. They commonly attend the school during the winter."* He did not *"think .. legislation .. necessary"* to prevent the employment of children. Vyner shared the attitude of a Government Minister, who, in 1862, said that education was not intended *"to raise children above their station and business in life .. but to give them an education that may fit them for that business."* Knight had noted in his logbook in January 1863 that *"several children commenced school after having been absent since the harvest."* It was, nevertheless, expedient to have some absentees, for, in March he found *"the First Class rather too large but think it will remedy itself by some of the children leaving off for spring work."* Advantage was not always taken of education due to inability to pay the penny a week charged for 'schooling'. The cost, the lack of clothing, and the need for children to work, all affected attendance.

The Later Victorian Era

In the 1870s, when some children started school very young and all left by 12 or 13 years of age, education concentrated on the '3 Rs' and school grants were determined on a payment by results basis. When Frederick Glover, a graduate in law and music and a Diocesan Inspector of Schools, arrived as rector in 1877 he did much to raise standards in the school. The appointment of Henry Hooper, a native of the Scilly Isles, as schoolmaster, and Mrs Hooper as assistant mistress, in 1888 led to a great improvement in the curriculum and standard of teaching. Attendance was then about 60-65 on average [the following year it was 94].

After the death of Thomas Knight in 1887, his son Charles opened a 'private adventure school' in Withern. Knight, who had assisted his father at the National School, does not appear to have been highly regarded by the rector and the new schoolmaster. About 15 pupils moved to his school, but his attempts to attract pupils were not very successful. Re-admittance to the National School was soon being sought - in October 1892 *"four children named Payne"* were admitted from Knight's school, which eventually disappeared without trace. The National School was, at this time, attended by children from Withern, Tothill and Woodthorpe. Strubby children attended a Parochial School for 40 children built in Strubby in 1878.

Health and Absence from School

Poverty and bad housing made the problems of sickness worse. Year after year there was illness in the village, particularly in the years 1863/4, 1873 and 1878. Mumps, measles, whooping cough, diphtheria, scarlet fever and typhoid fever were just some of the illnesses which regularly afflicted children [and grown-ups] in the village during the later years of the 19th century. Sometimes, as in 1896, social pressure was applied: "*Several children, on seeing [Lucy Watson] enter the play-ground, returned home. There are three cases of typhoid fever in her house. Although Dr Hanson said there was no risk .. thought advisable to tell her to absent herself for a time*." School was often suspended due to the prevailing infectious diseases - and the building cleaned and disinfected.

Illness was not the only cause of absence from school. A local sale, the Mablethorpe Show, the Wesleyan Sunday School outing, the Foresters' Feast, the Temperance Society's Tea, the Withern Horticultural Show, a Royal wedding or jubilee – all meant an official school holiday [no holiday usually meant unofficial absence of pupils]. Pea-picking was also a contentious matter, the Attendance Officer upbraiding Mr Marshall in 1892 for illegally employing 6 children who should have been at school.

The Slayton Years

After the departure of the Hoopers in 1894 the school was run for 30 years by George Slayton, a much respected man, whose untimely death in 1924 robbed Withern of an ardent supporter.

Education became effectively compulsory in 1880 and free in 1891. When Annie Clark went to school in 1903 'schooling money' no longer had to be paid. Lessons were also better conceived. While she spent most of her time learning reading,

1907.
Augt 23rd

Broke up after morning school for the
Harvest Holidays – six weeks.
During the past fortnight the school has
been examined in the work as set out
in the scheme and the results noted.
Just before closing this morning the Rev^d
C.N.Swayne presented "Perfect Attendance"
medals and certificates, for the year
ended April 30th, 1907, to the children
whose names follow:–
Gilt medal.(Two year's regular attendance).
    1. A.E.Slayton.
Bronze Medals (one year's regular attend^{ce})
    1. Annie Clark.   2. George Clark.
    3. Ernest Lane.   4. Herbert Lane.
    5. Alice Dixon.   6. Lily Dixon.
    7. Herbert Stones.
Certificates (Infants').
    1. Elizabeth Bullivant. 2. Wm Marshall.
    3. Rosannah Fawcett. 4. Frank Lane.

Average for week. 64·6.   Percentage, 88·4.

1907.
Octr 7th

Reopened school.   No. present. 644 am & pm.
Miss Dorothy Enderby, who has been
monitress since October 5th, 1903, has
been made a Supplementary Teacher.
The managers have, during the holidays,
placed in the big room two apex
ventilators and three air inlets.
The Revd C.N.Swayne took his class
in catechism this morning.

Octr 11th
Average for week. 66·7. Percentage, 88·9.
The Attendance Officer visited the
school on Tuesday, and also on Thursday.

Octr 14th
A wet day. Six children arrived in
such a wet condition that they had
to be sent home to change their clothing.

Octr 16th
The Attendance Officer called.

Octr 18th
Average for week, 69·8. Percentage, 94·3.

Octr 21st
The cesspool attached to the girls' offices
was filled in on Friday, and its place
taken by some sanitary pans.

Octr 23rd
The Revd C.N.Swayne visited the school
and heard the middle & upper
divisions read.

An extract from Mr Slayton's School Log Book, Autumn 1907. The rectors
always took an active interest in the life and work of the school.
[Reproduced by permission of Lincolnshire Archives]

School: Younger pupils with Mr Slayton and Miss Eva Webster, 1902.

Class I pupils with Mr Slayton, 1923.

writing and arithmetic, Annie also did embroidery, needlework [with a special needlework teacher], drawing [she recalled sketching *the lovely cherry trees*" in the Marshalls' garden at the Red Lion], and some singing - mainly hymns - with Miss Dorothy Enderby from The Manor. There were no organized games.

The children went to church on ceremonial occasions, such as Royal Jubilees and Coronations. In 1902, to mark the Coronation of King Edward VII and Queen Alexandra, they attended a service in church, then walked in procession through a gate and across to Withern Hall. Here Mrs Wells of Fishpond House presented each child with a commemorative mug, which was then used at a tea party, given in a wagon shed, before being washed and taken home.

In June 1911 "*The Rev CN and Mrs Swayne visited the school and presented each of the children with a medal as a souvenir of their Majesties' Coronation.*"

Patriotism and Empire came to dominate school life in the years up to the Great War. As early as 1873 Thomas Knight had given "*the little ones a good drilling in 'country'*". In 1912 Mrs Christison, of Burwell Park, addressed the children on 'Patriotism', presented the school with a 'Union Jack' and left five shillings for the scholar who should write the best essay on her address. A flag-staff for the flag was provided by the School Managers and, on Empire Day, the children saluted the flag and sang patriotic songs in place of their scripture lesson.

The Great War

The patriotic fervour of the 1900s must have been muted by the time the Great War reached its peak, the anxiety across the country being reflected in a February 1916 entry in the logbook: "*Admitted F & J Harrison [infants], grandsons of Mr G Harrison, who have come from Scunthorpe to stay with their grandfather to be out of the way of Zeppelin raids.*" The family was well-advised. When a Zeppelin bombed Cleethorpes Baptist Chapel in the following month, 31 members of the Manchester Regiment battalion billeted there were killed.

Pupils, like schoolchildren around the country, contributed to charity and the war effort. Scarves and mittens knitted by the girls and scarves "*knitted by some of the bigger boys*" were sent to the Red Cross; 'thank you' postcards for gifts of cigarettes arrived from soldiers of the Mesopotamia Expeditionary Force. In July 1916, as news came through of the horrific casualties being incurred in the Battle of the Somme, "*Mr S Marsden, of the Louth depot of the National Egg Collection for sick and wounded sailors and soldiers, called and thanked the children for the work they had done in connection with the collection.*" But the horror of war touched the school, 9 of the 14 local men who died on military service being 'old boys'. The anniversary of the Armistice was observed in silence on 11 November 1919. On 24 November - Louth Martinmas Fair - many children were absent!

A feature of the early 20th century was the falling number of children in the school's catchment area. There were 114 children on the books in 1894, but only 62 in 1914; in 1918 there were 63. Strubby's parochial school, which could accommodate 34 pupils, only had 22 in 1913.

An era ended when George Slayton, already ill by 1919, died in Louth Hospital in 1924; for his funeral the "*scholars .. formed a funeral party at the Churchyard.*" A fortnight after the funeral school was back to normal, Albert Crawford dislocating his right knee playing in the school yard at morning break.

School: Capt. Brown [left] with a group of older pupils c1928

The Juniors with Miss Mary Lowis, 1944.

1924-48

Frank Brown, a disciplinarian who had served as an officer in the Great War, became the Withern schoolmaster in 1924 and lived in the School House. Alice Slayton, who had run the school while her father was in hospital, went to be schoolmistress at Strubby. In the logbook Brown noted that the school was "*attended by children of all grades from two villages. Senior pupils also attend from a third village [Strubby] and a fourth is about to contribute in a like degree. It thus partakes of the nature of a rural central school. The programme of work has been compiled on thoughtful lines .. its theoretical side .. sufficiently wide, but [there are] no facilities .. for the practical instruction of either the boys or girls.*" Sport, especially football, was an outlet for youthful exuberance and Brown ran a school football team in the 1920s. Although known as 'Bossy' Brown, his view was that pupils should "*be increasingly dependent on their own efforts.*"

In addition to the usual English, reading and arithmetic lessons, pupils were given woodwork and cookery lessons from about 1934. Two woodworker benches with removable table tops arrived at the school and George Lowis, as the village carpenter's son, was detailed to teach woodwork! Eventually, the senior boys went once a week by bus to Mablethorpe for a woodwork lesson.

The older boys also had gardening lessons every week, there being three gardens in the 1930s - one in the school grounds, one at the back of the school and one at the Rectory. Instruction was given in crop rotation. Drawing and the study of nature, especially the flora in the environment of the school, were also important and there were weekly nature lessons and walks down to the river - when the less attentive ones were inclined to wander off!

By 1938 the prospect of war loomed again and in December the School, with "*some guests from Leeds*", gave a concert of Christmas carols, songs and dances, small plays and poems in aid of "*Comforts for the Lincolnshire Regiment*".

The school remained 'all-age' until 1948, pupils attending between the ages of 5 and 14. Organized in three parts, in 1939 Captain Brown and Freddie Ladds taught the senior class, Mrs Barr [from Gayton] the juniors and Miss White [from Maltby] the infants. The old cottage which adjoined the school had a woodwork room, and was used for the girls' cookery lessons. The relatively easy-going way of life enabled Lol Patchett to become a Telegram Boy while he was still attending school - Fred Jackson paying him 6d to deliver each telegram received at the post office!

Frank Brown retired at the beginning of World War II and Jim Elliott became the last head teacher of Withern's 'all-age' school.

Time of Change

The 1944 Education Act came into effect in 1948 and the school became a primary school within the state-maintained sector, retaining its affiliation to the Church of England. By 1951/52 Lindsey County Council had taken control of the School from the Church. Whereas all who attended the School had previously received religious instruction from the Rector on his regular visits, those who wished to do so were now allowed to opt out of religious instruction. The School, which took pupils from Gayton, Strubby, Tothill and Woodthorpe, had been receiving the pressing attentions of all the clergyman involved!

Celebrating the centenary of the National School, 1950.

The school 1973 with [left] Mrs Howard [Head Teacher] and Mrs Nicholson, and [right] Mrs Barr and Mrs Julian.

The children from Woodthorpe, Longlands and Stain came to school in Joe Perkins' taxi in the 1950s, when about 75 pupils attended. There were two classrooms – one for the infants and a large room [with a screen across it] for the older pupils. A canteen, built in the 1940s, but knocked down some years ago, was also used for lessons each morning before becoming the dining room for the meals cooked in the school kitchen.

As the new educational era took shape, in 1950 the School celebrated the 100th anniversary of its rebuilding as a National School, although it was already probably 150 years old.

THE HEAD TEACHERS AT WITHERN SCHOOL SINCE 1835

1835	Samuel Parrish
1840-50	William Elger
1850-87	Thomas Uriah Knight
1887-88	Mark Worth
1888-95	Henry Barnard Hooper
1895-1924	George Henry James Slayton
1924-40	Frank Brown MC
1940-48	James Elliott [c1942-46: Mr Gardner, acting head]
1948	Mrs Fade, acting head
1948-50	Miss Marjorie Smith [Maltby-le-Marsh]
1950	Miss Tate, acting head
1951-53	Miss Teasdale [Louth]
1954-62	Mrs Hilda Cunnington
1962-69	Miss Gladys Smith
1969-80	Mrs Winifred Howard
1980-84	Mrs Betty Sykes
1984	Mr Higgins, acting head
1984-92	Gerry Blythe
1992-	Mrs Valerie Kemp

Louis, Elsie and Bernard Dobson

Chapter 10:
The Village 1800-1875

End of an Era

Although the Fitzwilliams had gone and the Withern Feast, a traditional, probably rowdy, summer occasion celebrated on St Margaret's Day, had been discontinued in 1796, early 19th century Withern was still a backward 18th century parish.

Withern Hall and the Manor were tenanted farms and there was little of social consequence. The rector lived over twenty miles away, leaving the parish in the hands of a curate; the fabric of the mediæval church was crumbling; and farming still operated partly under the mediæval open-field system. Families endured poor conditions in their mud and stud homes, babies and mothers often dying during and after childbirth. Only the fittest survived.

Population Growth

The population of Lincolnshire more than doubled between 1801 and 1881. In Calcewath Hundred in 1801 only Alford, Mumby, Hogsthorpe, Willoughby and Bilsby had more inhabitants than Withern. Withern's population then comprised 66 families living in 52 houses [in 1718 there had been 43 families and recipients of alms living in the 'Town's Houses']. Of the 295 inhabitants, 46% were male. There were more people under 20 years of age and fewer inhabitants over 60 than there are today. In 1821 the number of families was the same, but the population had grown by nearly 50 and the number of houses by only 2! Such overcrowding was made worse by outbreaks of disease, such as cholera which occurred in Lincolnshire in 1830-32.

By 1841 Withern's population had risen to 435, nearly 48% being under 20 years of age and 54% male. The balance had shifted as more boys found work in Withern and more girls went away into service. Woodthorpe in 1841 had 9 inhabited houses and 55 inhabitants [60% male], 31 being under 20 years of age; all had been born in Lincolnshire.

Balance was restored by 1861, the population reaching its highest ever level - 528 - an increase of 80% since 1801. By 1871 it had declined to 452.

Almost all Withern's residents had been born in Lincolnshire in 1851, but only 44% had been born in Withern; of the heads of households, less than 20% were native to the parish. By 1861, when the population peaked, the proportion of heads of household born in Withern had risen to 23%, with a further 16% born in Claythorpe, Gayton, Strubby or Tothill.

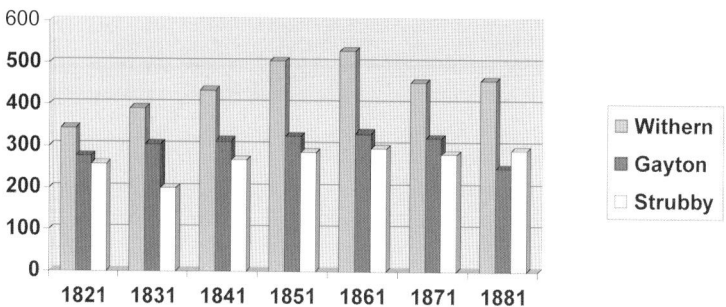

The populations of Withern, Gayton and Strubby compared 1821-81

While Withern's population grew in 1821-31, Strubby's decreased, 40 people emigrating. In 1827 the Strubby Vestry paid for Richard Harness, Matthew Smith and Christopher Jacklin and, in 1831, for William Ainsworth - and their families - to emigrate to "America"; several of the Jacklin and Ainsworth children were under 4 years old. Christopher Jacklin's descendants live in Ontario.

Over 60% of the heads of household in 1861 came from further afield. Examples of 'incomers' and movement were:

Uriah Fenwick, a 46 year old shepherd, who lived in Catley's Row in 1851 and Woodthorpe in 1861: born in Manby, his wife Ann born in Somersby, their children in Louth, Welton-le-Wold, Scamblesby and Withern;
and
John Parrish, an agricultural labourer, who lived in a cottage next to Willows Farm in 1861: born in Gayton-le-Marsh, his wife Ann born in Allington, their children in Hagnaby [aged 11, 10 and 8], Marshchapel [6], Great Carlton [4] and Withern [2].

Withern, a place to which people came to work, had a resident policeman, PC George Beadon, by 1861.

Housing

The growth in population was not matched by the increase in the number of homes. There were 52 houses in 1801, 64 [1 empty] in 1811 and only 54 in 1821. Demolition of houses obviously occurred in 1811-21, probably the removal of worn-out mud and stud cottages. The number of homes, including empty ones, increased after 1821 - by 25 [1831], 11 [1841], 6 [1851] and 13 + 3 under construction [1861].

New houses included:
- Catley's Row, Chalk Lane [Pump Cottage], 1830s;
- Wilson's Row [Cook's Cottages], 1840s;
- Woodlands, Chalk Lane, c1847-50;
- three houses between the shops [Wharfedale Cottage], 1850s;

'Withern Cottage', seen after the removal of its brick cladding and pantile roof; it was subsequently removed to Church Farm Museum, Skegness.

Miss Bratley in front of Virginia Cottage [now known as 'Three Acres'] c1914. This property belonged to John Stephenson, the market gardener, in the 1830s.

- six Stovin Maw "cottages" [eg Grange Farm Cottage], 1851-55;
- four houses on Main Road [Rose Cottage/Westfield House], 1860s;
- Wells Cottages [first Ramscroft houses], 1860s;
- two houses on Main Road [Colcroft House], c1862;
- Flaxmill Cottage, c1872;
- four houses next to the Methodist Chapel, c1875;
- two houses on the drive to Park Farm, 1870s.

Among the properties removed were:
- a cottage in front of the Poor Houses [where William Chantrey the shoemaker had lived], 1850s;
- John Cotton's cottage at the Main Road/Stain Lane junction, 1870s;
- White's carpenter's shop, on the site of Wells Close, demolished after 1876 when Thomas Graves moved the business to the former Three Tuns Inn. The Housing/Families balance in Withern 1801-71, as given in Census Reports

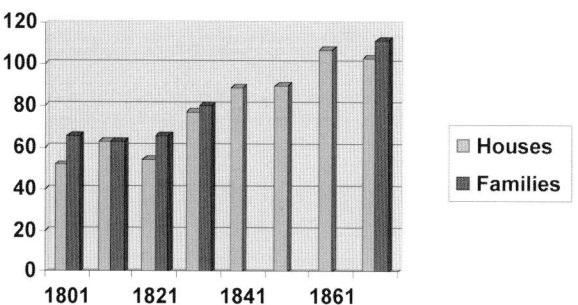

**The Housing/Families balance in Withern
1801-71, as given in Census Reports**

Withern needed tidying up. The Poor Houses, owned by the Churchwardens and Overseers of the Parish, stood in the centre of the village - two terraces between the Three Tuns and the Alms Houses, and a third across the road between Red Lion Farm and the Post Office. The Pinfold, where stray animals were impounded, was in front of what is now Red Lion Farm yard. The road was narrower and some Poor Houses stood in front of other properties. A decision by the Parish Vestry in 1843 to remove one terrace of Poor Houses was not implemented, probably because of increasing population and poverty - William Kennington's failure to pay his Poor House rent was discussed at a Vestry Meeting.

Some who were left alone, or became infirm, finished their days in the workhouse. John Cotton, a widower of 81, who had lived in a cottage at Grange Corner, was in Louth Workhouse in 1861, along with 11 year old Chris Broddle, son of William and Elizabeth Broddle, a couple who had been living in Withern in 1851.

In 1860 parts of the front gardens were taken from the Poor Houses between the Three Tuns and Chalk Lane to widen the road. Finally, in 1868, a Public Meeting decided to sell "the vacant land on which the poor houses stood, which have been pulled down .." The Poor Houses had gone at last.

The Red Lion Inn c1905; in Kelly's Directory 1900 the Red Lion offered "good accommodation for cyclists."

The western end of the village c1908. Beyond Woodford/Dayburgh [left], can be seen the old house at Daros, once occupied by Joseph Storey, the butcher, and behind it the Forge. Ladies are chatting in the road. Homeleigh [right] is thatched.

Red Lion Cottages, front view, with the Alms Houses visible in the background. Photographed in 1950 by MW Barley. [Reproduced by permission of Mrs D Barley/English Heritage. NMR]

Red Lion Cottages, back view, looking towards the newly built Vyner Row. Photographed in 1950 by MW Barley. [Reproduced by permission of Mrs D Barley/English Heritage. NMR]

Poverty

Parish Vestries ensured that no-one became a charge on a parish who had not been born in the parish. Examples of removals are:

1815:   John Smith, his wife and family, removed from Bilsby to Withern.

1830:   Thomas Smith and his young family, removed from Wainfleet to Withern.

1843:   Robert Brocksum, his wife and four small children, removed from Theddlethorpe St Helen to Withern;
and
Robert Atkin, his wife and four small children, removed from Withern to Tothill.

1861:   Lucy Desforges, a native of Withern and widow of Joseph Desforges, removed to Withern by Hannah cum Hagnaby as unable to support herself and family.

Some were a recurring problem. John Ross had been employed and paid for a whole year by the Stovin estate in about 1774, since when he had not *"done any act to gain a settlement elsewhere"*. After serving some days in the Louth House of Correction for vagrancy in 1813, it was ordered that he should be removed to the Parish of Withern. The House of Correction at Kirton repeated the exercise in 1817.

The Parish Vestry was controlled by the Rector, the doctor and the larger farmers - the ones who bore the brunt of parochial rates levied to support those needing help. The doctors, for those who could afford their services, were John Calvert c1822-46 and William C Calthrop MRCS from 1847.

Roads

The routes to Alford and Louth are, of course, ancient. In the 16th century the *"Alford gaite"* may have followed a more direct route towards Alford, passing to the east of Woodthorpe Hall, because there was then a "low gaite" to Woodthorpe. The *"low gaite"* appears to have become the route to Alford when the south-western section of the South Field was enclosed in the 17th century.

In the 16th century Stain Lane was the *"lowe gaite"* to Stain through the North Field. After the enclosure of the area known as The Intake between Barfen and Longlands Cottage the further section of Stain Lane was called 'the Intack lane'; from Longlands Cottage to Stain it was 'the Stain lane'.

Peters Lane is probably named after an 18th century person; a 'Peter's Onset' adjoined the lane.

Today's Chalk Lane was known for over 100 years as 'the Doctor's Lane'; in the 17th century it may have been the lane called 'Cotton lane' in a property deed.

Church Lane, occasionally called Mill Lane in Victorian times, was known as the *"Churche layne"* in 1601.

Gold Lane has been known by this name since at least the 18th century.

The 'Market road', which existed in the South Field in the 18th century, disappeared with the enclosure of the open field. The 'Toft road' in the East Field suffered the same fate, although 'Calfen lane' survived.

The sale notice of a South Reston farm in 1796 refers to "*a good Turnpike Road through the parish from the Town of Louth from which place there is a navigable Canal to the River Humber.*" Apart from the Louth road the 18th century roads were tracks for horses, wagons and farm implements to get to and from the fields; when Thomas Paine was the exciseman in Alford in 1764 the roads in the neighbourhood were said to have been deep and often under water.

The public roads were maintained by the Parish Vestry and covered in Spurn Gravel or chalk from South Thoresby. In 1844 it was agreed that the road from Woodthorpe Hall to Aby Road corner be "*covered with chalk from Thoresby*" and that "*from Mr Coulam's out gate to the Cow Close corner be repaired with Spurn Gravel.*"

In the centre of the village the road was widened in 1860 and in 1868 the roads from Mablethorpe to the village [Peters Lane], to the 'East Field', and to 'Longlands' were repaired with gravel. Chalk was used:

- on the main road to Cotton's corner [Grange Corner];
- from 'Cotton's corner' to Barfen lane;
- and from Barfen lane to the 'Bullrails'.

The surviving section of the old Woodthorpe Hall to Aby Grange road ['the Woodthorpe road'] was covered with Spurn Gravel - the road and houses on its northern side were in Withern parish.

Although the lane from Withern to Stain was maintained in reasonable condition, the Stain to Mablethorpe road was a grass track, remaining so until the 1930s; Joe Perkins once became stuck in the ruts at Stain Bridge in his Model T Ford.

The 19th century had few rules of the road and accidents occurred. In 1840 Dr Calvert, returning one afternoon from Louth market in a gig, knocked down an infirm old lady near the Boar's Head in Newmarket and failed to stop. The lady suffered injuries to her legs. Summoned before the Mayor of Louth, Calvert was urged by the Mayor to "*retire and compromise the affair,*" which he did, paying the lady £4 as recompense. Afterwards he "*applied to the Mayor to use his influence in preventing its being published in the papers* " - this from a man with four illegitimate children by three women!

Main Street, Withern in the 1930s

70

Chapter 11:
The People Before 1875

Surnames

Many surnames have been associated with Withern, albeit sometimes only briefly. "George the Traveller", buried in 1694, had no name. Paul Thorndike, whose daughter Martha was baptized in 1635, had a familiar one.

Of the 94 heads of household in Withern in 1851 only 20 had been born in Withern or Woodthorpe, the names being:

Bontoft, Bricksom, Bullivant, Cotton, Coupland, Desforges, Enderby, Grant, Kennington, Kirman, Maidens, Orry, Simpson, Swinn, Tickler, Topliss and White.

Many of these surnames arrived in Withern during the 18th century; few are found in Withern today. People moved around seeking work, often finding jobs at the annual hirings in Louth, and there was constant movement of families in Withern, Gayton and Strubby.

Trades

Although 70% of families in the parish were still engaged in agriculture early in the 19th century, in the 1820s Withern was becoming a busy commercial centre, much more so than its neighbours. The important resident village craftsmen - the tailor, the blacksmith, the carpenter/wheelwright and the boot and shoe maker – were all in Withern. Tailors and bootmakers went to the farms to measure and supply their products, a practice which still existed in the 1900s. There were also, of course, those who travelled around. Abraham Harrison, who was buried in Withern in 1829, was a 75 year old "itinerant peddler." Joseph Smith, "*a gypsy from the heath south of Lincoln, died in the lane*" in 1842.

Among those who plied their trades in Withern were:

Tailors: Mark Talkes [1630], Thos Harrison [18th cent], Christopher Harrison, a cottager [late 18th cent], William Kennington [1820s], John Bell [1830s] and John Wakelin [1840s]. Thomas Askey, born in Tothill, was a tailor for over 40 years, as was his son, William Gresswell Askey.

Blacksmiths: James Drury [1750s], George Young [1820s] and the Simpsons. Nicholas Simpson [d 1809] was a master blacksmith at the Old Forge in the 1760s. His son, Nicholas II [1776-1851], followed him and was at the centre of village life for forty years. Grandson Nicholas III [1807-67] and his widow continued the family tradition until the 1870s.

Carpenters: William Chantrey, John Spence and George Swinn [18th cent], Robert Bullivant [early 19th cent] and the Whites. John and Thos White were carpenters & wheelwrights, who worked at the Wells Close site; the business was taken over by Thomas Graves in the 1860s. James Risdal was a master carpenter & wheelwright at Three Acres in 1871.

Boot and Shoemakers: William Barker, master cordwainer [boot & shoe maker], born Alford, married a Withern girl, Theodosia Bontoft, in 1824, and opened a shop on Main Road between Hollydene and Brookfield, where he was still making shoes in 1885. Other shoe makers included: Edward Orry [the grocer], James Bontoft, James Broddle, William Chantrey and William Earl [1830s], and John Fitzpatrick [1840s]. Charles North, a journeyman shoemaker from Louth, who lived next to Red Lion Farm in 1851, had been making shoes in Withern since the 1830s. Sam Sivel, master boot & shoemaker, came to Withern c1870.

Other trades included: bricklayer [Joseph Catley, who was in Withern in the 1800s, and George Allett, born in Strubby, and his son William Allett]; builder [John Tatam]; saddler [Charles Bean, a Londoner]; milliner [Elizabeth Askey]; and dressmakers [Mary Knight, Margery Simpson, Thirza Tyson and Sophia Wright].

Thrashing Machine Operators: Joseph Coulam and William Jarvis [1830s] and Adlard and Benjamin Simons [1840s]. The Simons brothers, who lodged with the Risdal family at Peters Lane/Main Road corner in 1851, operated machines in Withern for over 30 years.

Market Gardening: Before 1838 John Stephenson, from Bilsby, bought Three Acres, where he ran a market gardening business for many years. His second cousin, Isaac Mountain, son of Sibright Mountain [a Bilsby glazier, born in Saleby], was a master gardener living in Gayton in 1861. In 1859-62 Isaac acquired part of Coal Croft, the field between the present Chapel and The Old Forge, where his sons Henry and Edly developed a very successful market garden.

The proportion of families engaged in trades and crafts rose from 25% in 1811 to 29% in 1831.

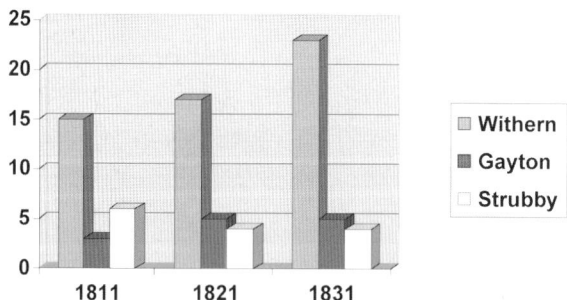

Number of families engaged in trade in
Withern, Gayton and Strubby 1811-31

Even in 1851 trade accounted for over 25% of employment in Withern in a higher population. Occupations varied. There were jobs for men on the farms, but fewer for women, who, if they were not doing back-breaking jobs in the fields, became cooks, dairymaids, housemaids and nursemaids; the lucky ones with experience might find jobs as housekeepers at rectories or large farms. William Brocksum, John Coupland, John Keal and James Taylor were *"labourers employed on the highways"*,

Joseph Coney a brewer's labourer and Joseph Whattam a jobbing gardener. William Risdale became groom and valet to the rector. Anne Fenwick and her daughter Ellen were laundresses.

People did any work that brought in money. John Chapman, who came from Maltby-le-Marsh, was publican at the Three Tuns in 1851, but also worked as a shepherd while his wife Naomi ran the inn and their smallholding. James Taylor, a 72 year old native of Gayton, was a Chelsea Pensioner. Although John Mawer's flax mill on the Aby Road failed in the Agricultural Depression, it added variety to the local scene for a time with Irish and Scots employees.

The Early Shops

There was probably a shop in Withern in the 17th century. Among the shops during the 18th century, when 'grocers' and 'drapers' sold virtually anything, were butchers John Gresswell, Thomas Odlin and Thomas Place and 'shopkeeper' Thomas Dales. In the 1790s and 1800s John Wright was a grocer & draper and Joseph Storey a butcher.

The Gresswell, Wright and Storey businesses continued into the 19th century, Ann Gresswell [pronounced 'Gressel' in the 18th century] running her family's shop after the death of her husband William in 1798. After Ann's death in 1820 William Gresswell jr took over; he was a grocer & druggist in 1835. Although William was educated [he could read and write], the business failed in his hands at a time of expansion generally in the village. He left Withern in the late 1840s; in 1851 he was a "pauper, Ag Lab" living with his family in Dales Terrace in Louth.(17)

The existence of drapers and haberdashers reflected the degree to which dresses, shirts, night attire, household linen and furnishings were sewn at home. Suits, coats and footwear were the preserves of tailors and shoemakers - the last trades in which producers and consumers dealt directly with each other. The Village Stores proprietor was a grocer and draper throughout the 19th century and the Supply Stores developed along the same lines.

The 'Village Stores' buildings [now houses] contain traces of mud and stud. As noted earlier, Edward Orry held religious meetings in a building erected "*before 1800*", which suggests that the 'Village Stores' may have been the shop of Thomas Dales and John Wright before it was taken over by Maddison Orry. Dales, who was described as a "proud shopkeeper" in the Withern parish register in 1760, died in 1795. Wright was a grocer and draper until his death in 1808. As Maddison Orry was in Withern in 1809 it seems likely that he took over Wright's premises.

In 1835 Thomas Askey, who had married a sister of William Gresswell jr in 1823, had his tailor & draper's shop at Hollydene. Joseph Catley, the bricklayer, was also a grocer & draper for a time. Richard Johnson dealt in earthenware.

Trade expanded. Richard Young, grandfather of Joseph Wilson Farrow of Strubby, took over William Taylor's butcher's shop at Homeleigh in the 1830s. Edward Tickler was a grocer near the site of the Alms Houses; Edward Fenwick, a farm worker, became a grocer; and John Larder was a grocer and draper.

As the population increased, more traders arrived. The shops opened by William Barker, the shoemaker, and Thomas Askey, the tailor, were joined in the late 1840s by a post office [probably at the rear of the present Post Office] run by Rebecca Desforges, Joseph Storey's daughter.

Edward Orry, the grocer & draper, appears to have been an erratic character. A Primitive Methodist, he upset the members of the Parish Vestry on a bookkeeping matter! He left Withern in about 1856 and died in Alford in 1877. His wife and son, Maddison Wm Orry, carried on the business, young Orry becoming postmaster on the retirement of Rebecca Desforges in the 1860s.

Neighbouring parishes had more limited shopping facilities. Gayton had two shopkeepers in 1856 [William Mason and Jemima Rannard] and a tailor [Frederick Webster]'; Strubby only had one shopkeeper [Robert Janney]; Tothill had none. So people came to shop in Withern.

Thomas Askey had become a tailor, draper & grocer by 1858. His son, William Gresswell Askey, 'grocer, draper & druggist', took over the business of Thomas Cockett [a grocer & draper in the present Post Office premises in the early 1860s] before 1868, Thomas continuing as a tailor at Hollydene until his death in 1870.

By 1872 the 'retailers' were:
Maddison Wm Orry, grocer/draper/ postmaster;
William Gresswell Askey, grocer/draper/tailor;
Ellen Fenwick, general shopkeeper;
George Tickler, miller & baker;
William Barker and Samuel Sivil, shoemakers;
and Richard Young, Henry Webster and Thomas Carter, butchers.

Inns

There were two alehouses in Withern in the late 18th and early 19th centuries:

The Red Lion: 'The Red Lion', the heraldic emblazon of John of Gaunt, has long been used as a sign for inns [a Red Lion inn existed in Stony Stratford in the 1520s and one in Islington claimed to have existed since 1415]. John Spence, licensee in 1792, may have been at the Red Lion in Withern in 1780. When he died in 1802 the inn was taken over by Francis Barker, who remained for about thirty years. Thomas Marshall, from Belleau, who arrived in Withern c1827 as a farmer/butcher, took over The Red Lion c1831, Francis Barker continuing as a brewer. The inn was rebuilt in the 1860s and the Marshall family ran it until 1916.

The Three Tuns: 'The Three Tuns', the insignia of The Worshipful Company of Vintners in 1442, is another English inn name with a long history. While James Vear, a farmer and victualler who died in 1758, may have been landlord of The Three Tuns, John Upton certainly was in 1792. John Pocklington, licensee in 1803, remained until the 1830s when Joseph Heaton took over. John Chapman, born Maltby-le-Marsh, licensee in 1849, stayed until the late 1860s [when he died in 1890 he was buried at Strubby]. Alfred Lusby, the last landlord, saw the pub close c1876.

In Strubby there was an alehouse, the licensee in 1792 being Thomas Beels [guarantor for his application: John Ma(i)dens, a Mumby innkeeper] and in 1803 George Janney [guarantor: Thomas Frow of Mablethorpe]. In 1842 Isaac Teesdale had a 'beerhouse'.

The Temperance Movement

There were about 76,000 public-houses in the British Isles in 1790; by 1850 there were over 88,000. The increasing consumption of alcohol, and consequent drunkenness, led to the formation of temperance societies seeking to curb excessive drinking. Some people signed a pledge to abstain totally from alcohol. A Somerset member of the National Temperance League wrote that "*it was the practice [c1814] .. for shopkeepers to give beer and wine to their customers ..*" Whether this happened in Withern is not known, but it is hardly surprising that both The Independent Order of Rechabites, a temperance friendly society founded in 1835 and sometimes known as the 'disciples of the pump', and the Band of Hope, founded in 1847, found a following.

Rechabite Tents [branches] were formed in Strubby and Withern in about 1840. The short-lived Strubby branch met in Strubby Methodist Chapel, but the Methodist Church generally held back from teetotalism, members being divided on the issue. The movement was not at that time allowed to hold meetings in Withern Chapel. The 'Ebenezer Tent' in Withern appears to have been associated in the 1840s with the Primitive Methodists in the village, a correspondent reporting in the Stamford Mercury that "*the decree which denies the use of Wesleyan Chapels to Teetotallers, has aroused the latter to exertion here; they have fitted up a commodious building for their own use*" [this was probably Edward Orry's warehouse, which was used for Primitive Methodist services in the 1840s]. Men, "*once the disgrace of civilization,*" had "*by their temperate habits been raised to the sphere of industrious usefulness and respectability ..*"

The Tent received support from William Vyner, Christopher Taylor of Tothill Manor, and a number of farmers keen to assist their labourers to join. Game, fowls, pork, beef, cheese and butter were given by them towards one of the early Rechabite suppers. The donors may not all have been abstainers. As with education, there was undoubtedly a mite of self-interest on the part of the middle-class in raising standards of morality and behaviour among the labourers; certainly, some of the leading farmers later in the century needed temperance as much as their labourers.

Carriers

The journey to the markets in Alford and Louth was usually made on foot or by carrier's cart, the bus service of the day. In 1826 Moses Scrimshaw was carrier from the Red Lion in Louth and John Mawer carried between The Marquess of Granby in Louth and the Widebar Gate in Alford. Thomas Davy and James Stephenson were carriers to Louth every Wednesday in 1842; in the late 1840s William Baggaley was a carrier and coal dealer. The Strubby curate noted in 1843 that a four-horsed coach to Louth passed through Strubby every Wednesday and Saturday at 8 a.m., returning in the evening. William Carrott, who came to Withern c1860 as a labourer and married an Aby girl, bought a few acres in Peters Lane, where he built 'Carrott's Corner' and established himself as a carrier; by the 1870s he was going to Louth every Wednesday and Saturday.

Longevity

Life was hard and there was little help for those in distress. Many died from disease in overcrowded homes. Accidents also took their toll. David Johnson of Withern, "*a young man, highly industrious,*" according to the Rector, was killed by a fall from a wagon in 1757; and, in 1836, the Rector noted in the parish register that Solomon Copeland, who had died aged 15, had been "*accidentally slain*". But, despite the hazards, those who survived often had long lives:

John Broddle, a cottager, was 98; Michael Lancaster 93; John Burnet 90; Robert Lucas 90; Mary Watson 90; Mary Julian, of Woodthorpe, 89; George Allett 89; Mary Lill 88; and William Cotton 86.

George Jacklin was 100 years old when he died in 1829 in Strubby, where the curate observed that "the neighbourhood is notorious for old age and healthiness." Mrs Mayfield in Gayton was 102 in 1831.

Going Overseas

Emigration was one way out for frustrated young people and there are numerous examples of families from the area who sought new horizons overseas. Joseph Haw, born in Belleau, served in the Royal North Lincolnshire Militia 1798-1814 [during the Napoleonic Wars], settling in Swaby after his discharge; in 1827 he took his wife and children to Ontario, Canada, where his log cabin stood for 95 years. Paul Wilson from Withern and John and Hewson Paine from Maltby-le-Marsh settled at Lacolle in Quebec c1830. John Baldock of Authorpe, who married Sabina Bee in 1821, sailed for Australia in the ship 'Fairfield' in 1840 with his wife and numerous children. George Allis, born in Strubby in 1852, died in Colorado, USA, in 1899. John Cumberworth, son of John and Lydia Cumberworth of Withern [they lived in the Woodhouse Cottage on the Aby Road in 1851], who emigrated to the USA in the late 1850s, served in the 1st Ohio Independent Battery of Light Artillery in the American Civil War in 1862-65 and later became a tile manufacturer in Ohio. The Bruntletts from the Fen area of Great Carlton, went to the USA [young John Bruntlett was working with Thomas White, the Withern wheelwright, in 1841]. William Carter, a Withern carpenter, went to New Zealand in the 1870s. With his wife of two weeks, John Chapman [son of the Woodthorpe farmer who had been landlord of the Three Tuns in Withern] sailed for Australia in 1877 in the ship 'Garnock'.(18) All were seeking a better life.

Some of those who went to Australia were probably less enthusiastic emigrants. Thomas Young, a young man from Belleau, who was convicted of cutting and stealing hair from the tail of one horse and the manes from five horses, all belonging to William Cotcheifer, a Withern farmer, was transported to New South Wales for seven years in 1820. In 1836 John Bemrose of Sloothby, aged 35, grandson of Robert Lucas of Woodthorpe, stole a waist-coat, for which he was tried at Lindsay Quarter Sessions. Found guilty, he was transported to New South Wales for seven years, sailing from London a year later. His wife, Diana Dunnington from Authorpe, never re-married and died in Willoughby about thirty years later.

One local man even made his living roaming the world. Captain Will Burkitt was master of the ship 'Teddo'; his first wife, Mary [daughter of William and Elizabeth Kelk of Woodthorpe, and sister of George Kelk of Manor Farm], who sailed with him, died "at sea during her passage from China to England" in September 1862, aged only 20. She is commemorated on a gravestone near the entrance to Strubby Church. Their son, William Kelk Burkitt, baptized in Shanghai in January 1862, was raised by the Kelk family at Woodthorpe Hall and attended Withern School. The Captain continued his travels, his children by his second wife being educated by a governess in the family home in Hamilton Place, Alford in 1881: Agnes and Alicia had been born in China; Joseph in "Isle St Antonio"; and Elizabeth in Alford.

Chapter 12:

A Busy Time 1875-1920

The Foresters

This was the heyday of the Ancient Order of Foresters in Withern, a time when the popular virtues of thrift and self-help produced a huge growth of friendly societies, co-operative societies and trade unions. A centre of trade, with strong nonconformist influence and reasonable employment opportunities, Withern was fertile ground for the Foresters and the Rechabites, who had no difficulty in attracting members.

A branch of the Foresters, known as Court 'Good Intent' No 972, existed in Withern for over 100 years. Founded in 1840, it originally met in The Red Lion Inn. By 1869 the meeting place had moved to The Three Tuns Inn, but from 1871 the Order avoided licensed premises and met in "*the Schoolhouse*". The 36 members in 1845 had increased to 144 [and 5 honorary members] by 1896, when the Court had £1,338 in funds [it also owned a small field in Strubby in 1908]. Officeholders included William Risdal, Maddison Orry, William Carrott sr, George Tickler, William Mountain, Richard Atkin, William Carrott jr, John Waby, W Watson, and CW Thorndike, reflecting a strong Methodist influence.

The Foresters were one of the societies approved to act as agents for the Government in operating the National Insurance scheme introduced in 1912. The Withern Court then had 138 State members, of whom 105 were also voluntary members. By the 1930s responsibility for the State members had been transferred to a special Court for State business run from Louth. This change, and the Depression of the 1920s and 1930s, led to a decline in membership by 1939. The Court closed shortly after World War II.

Celebration of the anniversary of a Foresters' Court was an occasion for great excitement, the band, resplendent in uniforms and sashes, leading a procession to the church. The school could not compete. The schoolmaster recorded in his logbook in 1863: "*School very small this morning - holiday in the afternoon - Foresters Feast*" and, from this date, the school closed every year until 1909 when "*Holiday - Foresters' Anniversary*" is recorded for the last time.

The Withern Court celebrated its anniversary in style in 1883. The Stamford Mercury reported members marching "*in procession through Maltby and South Reston [where many of the brethren live] to St Margaret's Church, Withern ..*" A Dinner was held and addresses given by the Rectors of Muckton and Theddlethorpe All Saints and the Vicar of Alford. The paper observed that "*perhaps no club in the neighbourhood is in so flourishing a condition ..*"

Population Decline

Withern's population decreased by 14% in the years 1861-71, 10% in 1891-1901 and over 10% in 1911-21. Some moved away to the towns; some emigrated, like Frederick Laking, who went to Canada, and young Walliss Thomas Wells, who went to Queensland, Australia, in the 1900s.

A group of Withern Foresters c1900.

Foresters' on Hospital Sunday c1905. A decorated cart, with William Clark holding the horse 'Jubilee' and William Carrott jr standing next to the cart. 'Hospital Sundays', held from the 1870s on the Sunday nearest St Luke's Day [18 October], were when churches had special collections for hospitals; the Foresters always played a major part in these events.

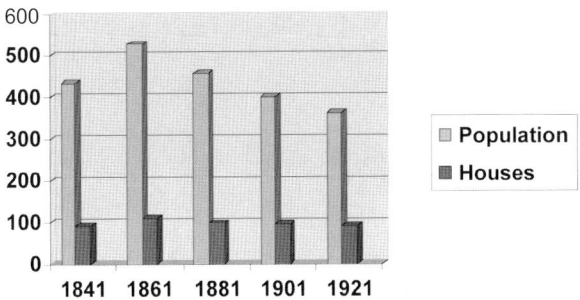

Changes in population and number of houses in Withern 1841-1921

Wages

Wages were never high and it is hard to imagine how people managed on the meagre amounts they received. In 1843 a maid could be hired for £4-10s-0d a year [8.65p a week] and a boy to help around the house and garden for £2-10s-0d a year [4.8p a week] and his board. Little changed over the next 70 years; even early in the 20th century a young farmworker received only 2s-6d [12.5p] a week. Girls were cheap domestic help, a nursemaid at one Withern farm receiving from her wages a penny each morning and a penny each afternoon - the rest being retained to pay for her keep! Her clothes were sent home to her mother to be washed. A girl general servant at a local farm in the 1930s received 2s-6d a week and her board.

Business

The trades changed. Askey's tailoring business ceased. John Hutton became the blacksmith. Thomas Graves, the carpenter at Sunnyholme, was succeeded by Charles Larder. John Waby, who took over the business in the 1890s, was the carpenter until after the Great War.

Samuel Sivil, the bootmaker, who died in 1913, was remembered by his Methodist Sunday School pupils as a big man with a hairy face, who loved the Book of 'Sammy-well'. His daughter-in-law took cloth woven in a weaving shed in the village [it stood where the Surgery now is] to Leeds where it was sold.

A 'rag and bone' man, William Atkin, lived in Peters Lane and itinerant tradesmen also called at Withern. As George Holmes wrote: "*the scissor grinders came, and the men who renewed a wicker chair bottom, and those who drilled tiny holes in broken china to repair it.*"

In the 1870s Adlard Simons retired to his small farm, Benjamin continuing the thrashing machine business at Maltby-le-Marsh, and by 1876 the Harrisons had taken over as the main thrashing machine operators in Withern. Cook Harrison, son of William Harrison, a Woodthorpe farmer, had established himself as a 'steam threshing machine owner' at North Thoresby in the 1850s. Moving to Fulstow, he and his sons developed a considerable business, including a brickyard. His brother Robert, who was also a 'well-sinker', stayed at the family farm at Woodthorpe.

Two of Cook's sons, George and William, came to Withern to run the new enterprise. In 1881 George, a driver, lived at Hollydene, the old Askey house; William, a steam engine maker or fitter, lived in Catley's Row. The engines were kept in a yard next to Hollydene.

James Woodliff, who lived in Orry's Yard, was also a thrashing machine proprietor.

Housing

More old houses disappeared. Thomas Davy's farm and some cottages in Chalk Lane were removed, as were the cottages next to Willows Farm. Off the Aby Road, close to Withern Wood, the Woodhouse Cottage was demolished. In the 1840s this had been the home of Thomas Marwood, who in old age lived with his daughter on the Alford Road.(19)

In 1881 there was a house, occupied by Matthew Horsewood, a cottager, in the small area of land between the main road and the parish boundary, near Strubby New Town. The house has gone, but one of its outbuildings stands in the smallholding on the site. A new house on Main Road [Meersbrook] became the 'police house'. PC Worsdale, who arrived as the resident policemen c1880, lived here for several years. Later occupants included PC Watson, who died in 1896, and PC Dobson, who was in Withern during the Great War.

Doctors

In the 19th century Withern had a series of very well qualified doctors. William McBeath followed William Calthrop, who died in 1872. A few years later James Hurley arrived. Edward Hull was the doctor in the 1880s and Alfred Hanson in the 1890s. George Hirst, doctor for a few years in the 1900s, was one of the instigators of the first Withern Show in 1901. When he left the district in October 1903, he was succeeded by Dr AAJ McNabb.

The Motor Car

Life was quieter in those days. The Rector rode in his carriage ["*one horse, not a pair*", said Mrs Jackson] to William Clark's house in Peters Lane to collect fruit and vegetables. The advent of the internal combustion engine removed the tranquillity. The first cars appear to have been those owned by the Revd Noel Swayne and Bill Odling, the Authorpe vet. In his diary Bishop Edward Lee Hicks notes that, on his arrival at Aby Station for a visit to Withern in 1913, "*Swayne met me in his little motor*." Alf Frankum, chauffeur to Dr McNabb, also an early car-owner, recalled driving a steam-powered car which had to be heated by a blow lamp!

Shops

The shops in the village began to change. The following is a short history up to 1920.

Supply Stores [Post Office]: William Askey was a grocer and draper here until his death in 1891, when WT Hardy took over. By 1900 it was 'The Acme Supply Stores' of John West, a 'grocer, draper, clothier, boot & shoe dealer'. JS Thorn, who came to the 'Supply Stores' c1904, obtained the Post Office contract in 1906. He was followed by GR Urry in 1912 and Walter Swaby in 1920.

Village Stores [corner of Gledhill Drive]: After Maddison Orry retired in 1896, the Village Stores/Post Office was run by Robert Willson, who married Minnie, daughter of Henry Webster, the Withern butcher. When Willson left Withern in 1906 to become the manager of Marsdens, a Nottingham grocery firm, the Post Office

Main Road, looking east, showing the old Methodist Chapel [left] and the new Chapel and the 'police house' [right] c1908.

Hollydene c1920 - the house and shop of the tailor Thomas Askey in the 1830s.

MAIN ST & POST OFFICE, WITHERN.

Main Road, looking west, Willson's Village Stores/Post Office [right], the former Three Tuns Inn [left] and 'Red Lion Cottages' in the background c1905.

Thorn's Supply Stores and Post Office c1908.

contract was transferred to the Supply Stores. Crowsons had the Village Stores for a time, Edwin Swaby following them c1910. Fred Jackson arrived in 1913. In Crowson's time, 'Gran' Jackson recalled a small cousin, who was staying there and playing in an upstairs part of the shop, finding and unplugging the treacle vat – his misdemeanour becoming apparent when treacle dripped through the ceiling into the downstairs room!

Fenwick's/Perkins: Edward Fenwick, and later his daughter Ellen [Nellie], had a general shop on the land between the chapel and Meersbrook. In 1897 Nellie acquired the old Chapel across the road, then a warehouse, from William Askey's trustees. Nellie died in 1912; although her grave bore the epitaph "*She thought more for others than herself*," it has been said that she was not over generous when serving customers! J W Perkins took over her shop, a corrugated iron building, and moved it to the eastern side of the chapel, the move being achieved one night by several sturdy men using poles to roll the building intact along the road; there was no disruption of trade! At the new, larger site he expanded into cars, bicycles and coal [Elijah Stones was a cycle agent/coal merchant at the Old Chapel before the Great War].

Butcher's Shop: In 1879 Richard Young, the butcher at Homeleigh, died. Henry Webster, who may have trained with Young, became the village butcher, based at Gold Lane [Failte], where he lived with his wife and her father William Jarvis. His business, which lasted about 30 years, became Carter's before and Norton's after the Great War.

Other traders: In 1892 these included James Wilson, provision dealer, and Thomas Watson, "shopkeeper and hawker". Watson, who had a shop in Peters Lane, at one time lived and had a shop at Homeleigh.

The Parish Council

Withern with Stain Parish Council was formed under the Local Government Act 1894. At its first meeting in that year the rector, the Revd FA Glover, was invited by the Council to chair its meetings, which he continued to do until his departure from Withern in 1907. The members of the first Council were: John Beels, William Carrott, Arthur Enderby, Henry B Hooper, John Thomas Marshall, John Mawer jr and Walliss Thomas Wells.

The Council met regularly before the Great War, but less often in the 1930s. Dormant during the 1939-45 War, it was revived in 1946 when the role of Clerk was taken on by Walter Swaby, who made considerable efforts to make the parish councillors aware of their responsibilities and the matters to which they should be directing their attention.

Church and Alms Houses

Despite the 1811-14 rebuilding of the church, a thorough restoration of the chancel was needed in 1875. Other changes may have been made at that time, for George Holmes wrote that a local man, born c1845, claimed to have "*built the south porch, the entrance [having been] formerly at the west end*". The condition of the church deteriorated again, however, and the interior had to be renovated and reseated in 1894. An extension of the churchyard, opened in 1908, met the needs of the 20th century, the first burial being of Sydney Walpole Gash, aged three months.

Annie Grant was the daughter of William Grant, who farmed at The Manor and later at Withern Hall before moving to Saltfleetby. She married Alphonse Pahud, from Switzerland, who taught French and Geman at Louth Grammar School. After her death in 1899 Alphonse was grief-stricken and in 1902 he committed suicide, leaving money to provide facilities for the residents of Louth and Withern [where he and Annie were buried]. In Louth Hubbards Hills were acquired by his Trustees and developed as a public park. In Withern they provided the Alms Houses, a new organ [built by Thomas S Jones & Son of London], a lectern and a communion table and service for St Margaret's Church; the organ is now at St Nicholas' Church, Addlethorpe.

The Great War

The years 1875-1914 were a most active period in Withern's history:
- Church and Chapel played major roles in village life and gave leadership;
- the rebuilt Red Lion provided a focal point and support for many events;
- Withern Show fostered horticultural competition [echoing Joseph Chamberlain's call for agricultural workers to have their own smallholdings - 'three acres and a cow']; and
- trades, shops and friendly societies flourished.

Sadly, though, during the years 1900-1919 Withern lost many important figures. Among those who died were Walliss Thomas Wells, the Revd FA Glover, Fred Tickler, John Wells, Sam Sivel, Richard Atkin, JT Marshall and William Carrott. Dr Hirst, Robert Willson, the Revd CN Swayne, Dick Marshall and William Walliss Wells left the parish.

The 1914-18 War had a dramatic impact: families lost sons who went to serve in the Army, Withern Show ceased, and the old order disappeared.   In 1914 the Parish Council organized a collection, raising £8-3-0 for the National Relief Fund, and a letter of appreciation was received from Buckingham Palace. The war involved the use of cavalry [and saddlers] and bicycles, and a company of cyclist troops was stationed in Withern. This must have fascinated the village youngsters - how different it was from today's warfare! Few villagers probably knew or cared that Richard Stovin Maw's grandson, Arthur Maw Mitchison, travelling in his Rolls-Royce in Germany on the day the Great War broke out, had his 40/50 hp landaulet-bodied motor requisitioned by the Germans [he sought compensation from the British Government!].

The Parish Council had other wars on its mind - wars on sparrows and rats – and, in 1917, offered 3d a dozen for sparrows' heads and 1d a dozen for their eggs. Dick Marshall was in charge.

Rantanning

The leading players in village life were not always popular. Mrs McNabb, the doctor's wife, effectively bent villagers to her will. To some she was kind [if you were 'church' you tended to receive favours; if you were 'chapel' it was less likely], but her rough treatment of people was legendary and her control of events remarkable. On one memorable occasion during the Great War her action led to a crowd of young men gathering in the field opposite her house and 'rantanning' her – a tradition in which shouting, hooting and the 'tin pot band' [discordant banging of tin pans, horns and other objects] made the offender well aware of popular opinion! (20) Attributed to two quite different incidents – her mistreatment/ eviction of a French girl who was living with the McNabbs or her peremptory dismissal of Alf Frankum, the doctor's chauffeur, who consequently lost his tied house - the action made clear that the villagers were not impressed.

William Clark and family at Twigmore Cottage [now known as Orchard Farm] c1903.

The cottages in the centre of the village c1905 [now one house known as Wharfedale Cottage]. [Reproduced by permission of North-East Lincolnshire Museums Service]

The Revd FA Glover, the musical rector.

Robert Willson, the village postmaster.

TG Tickler, son of George Tickler, the Withern miller;
founder of the Tickler jam manufacturing company.

JT (Tom) Sivil

Air view of the centre of Withern looking west, c. 1970

A quiet moment at Withern Bridge c1910.

Withern Band c1900. The players on this photograph were named by Mr JW Bullivant as [left to right] back row: Tom Sivil, - Willson, W Bullivant, Mark Rowe and John White; front row: John S, John Beels and Edly Mountain. [Reproduced by permission of North-East Lincolnshire Museums Service]

Chapter 13:

Recreation

Entertainment

In the 1900s agricultural workers still followed the narrow, traditional way of life found in country areas with estates. Old Mr Gowshall, who lived in retirement at The Old Forge, remembered how, in his youth, it had been customary to attend the Candlemas Market in Louth in February for the hiring. Sometimes, time off work could be arranged to attend the November Martinmas Fair, but there was little to spare from 2s-6d [12.5p] a week for entertainment and luxuries. He had been to the cinema once - unlike Mrs Rose Watson, who, in her life of over 100 years, had never been; she spent her spare time sewing and crocheting.

Commercial entertainment had not yet arrived, other than German bands performing at festivals and the Italian hurdy-gurdy man making his monkey dance on top of the organ. Young people looked forward eagerly to the annual Foresters' Festival and the July dancing festival on the first Saturday after St Margaret's Day, when they enjoyed dancing, swing-boats, coconut shies, skittles and music by a fiddler from Louth. More serious recreation was available at Dr McNabb's Red Cross classes.

That people enjoyed themselves there is no doubt, whether at festivals, or, as George Holmes wrote, celebrating with friends at Louth market and, on their return, losing their way in their horse and trap and ending up in Withern Wood.

A 'Coronation Festivities Committee' arranged the celebration of the Coronation of King Edward VII in 1902. There were the usual jollifications and flag waving and each pupil at the school received a commemorative mug. While there had not been a coronation for over sixty years, villagers had celebrated the Prince of Wales' Wedding Day in 1863, Queen Victoria's Golden Jubilee in 1887 and her Diamond Jubilee ten years later; in 1887 the school closed for both the anniversary and the 'Withern Jubilee Festivities' day.

Withern Show

"The most outstanding event of the year was the Flower Show, held in the inn field .. The exhibits reached a high standard, and there were amusements such as the shooting gallery and coconut shies, together with stalls for sweets, refreshments and ices. All along the village street flags were hung, and the inn yard was a feast of colour." [The Revd George Holmes]

The Withern and District Horticultural Society, founded at a meeting in the Red Lion Inn on 24 January 1901, was, from the start, a strong body. Ably run for the first three years by its Joint Secretaries - village doctor George Hirst and Robert Willson, the proprietor of the Village Stores, it was later well served by the schoolmaster, George Slayton, an excellent Secretary from 1905 to 1917, and his colleagues, first JW Arnott and later the Revd Noel Swayne. The first Chairman,

William Walliss Wells, was succeeded in 1903 by HD Addey, of Claythorpe, who remained Chairman for the rest of the Society's life. The Management Committee included:

W Oldroyd [Belleau]	JT Sivel	JS Thorn
H Holloway [Reston]	JT Marshall	H Millson [Claythorpe]
J Kelk [Woodthorpe]	H Webster	RA Rainthorpe [Tothill]
D Ball [Gayton]	F Searby.	

Rules established by the Committee required the Society's members to be inhabitants of Withern and the parishes of Aby, Authorpe, Beesby, Belleau, Claythorpe, Great Carlton, Little Carlton, Gayton-le-Marsh, Maltby-le-Marsh, South Reston, North Reston, Saleby, Strubby-with-Woodthorpe, South Thoresby and Tothill. The objects of the Society were to encourage the cultivation of flowers and vegetables and to hold a Show in Withern in the month of July.

The first Show, in 1901, was a resounding success. Lord Willoughby de Eresby, MP, came from London to open it and over 1,000 people attended. The weather was perfect, although heavy showers occurred elsewhere in the district. The Society's membership reached 127.

The Louth Advertiser reported that "*a most enjoyable day was spent at Withern*" in 1902, the Show being designed to avoid "*dullness and monotony*". "*Withern Brass Band .. enlivened the proceedings with selections during the afternoon and there was dancing in the evening.*" A ping-pong tournament, entertainment and a lecture on bee-keeping contrasted with a sports programme which included a 'bull fight' - "*men in sacks endeavouring to keep upright against the assaults of their co-contestants.*" Later years saw hockey on horseback, a pig-pelting competition and a baby show among the attractions, along with acrobats, Fred Clements' London Concert Party [Mablethorpe Section], The White Coons [minstrels from Mablethorpe] and a Punch & Judy show. When Withern Band was unable to attend, the Alford Excelsior Band played, except in 1912 when Mr W Barton's String Band from Louth provided the music.

By 1903 the press reported that "*the Withern exhibition has now attained a standard of unsurpassed excellence as a country show in north Lincolnshire*" – this in a year remarkable for "*a phenomenal amount of rain,*" which seriously affected horticulture. "*Beautiful summer weather*" again made Show Day a great success in 1904, despite a drought which had "*affected horticulture and floriculture in some instances far more adversely than the wet of last season.*" As on all festive occasions in those days, residents decorated the village and "*bannerettes arched the roadway.*" In 1906, a "*very hot summer*", the Gymkhana Contest had a Parachute and Cigar Race ['bring your own parachute'] and a combined 'Smock and Cap and Bending Race'! Attendance dropped in 1909; "*the weather, which had looked very threatening all day, broke up towards the evening, when there was a steady downpour of rain.*" Show Day in 1912, a very wet year, was "*unsettled*". At the 1914 Show, held a month before the Great War began, the honey, "*owing to the dry season, was not up to the standard,*" but the vegetables were of good quality.

Although still significant, support for the show, which had been highest in 1902-1908, had, in 1914, fallen below that for the first show in 1901. Several of the original enthusiasts had died or left the area; this, and the effect of the war on life

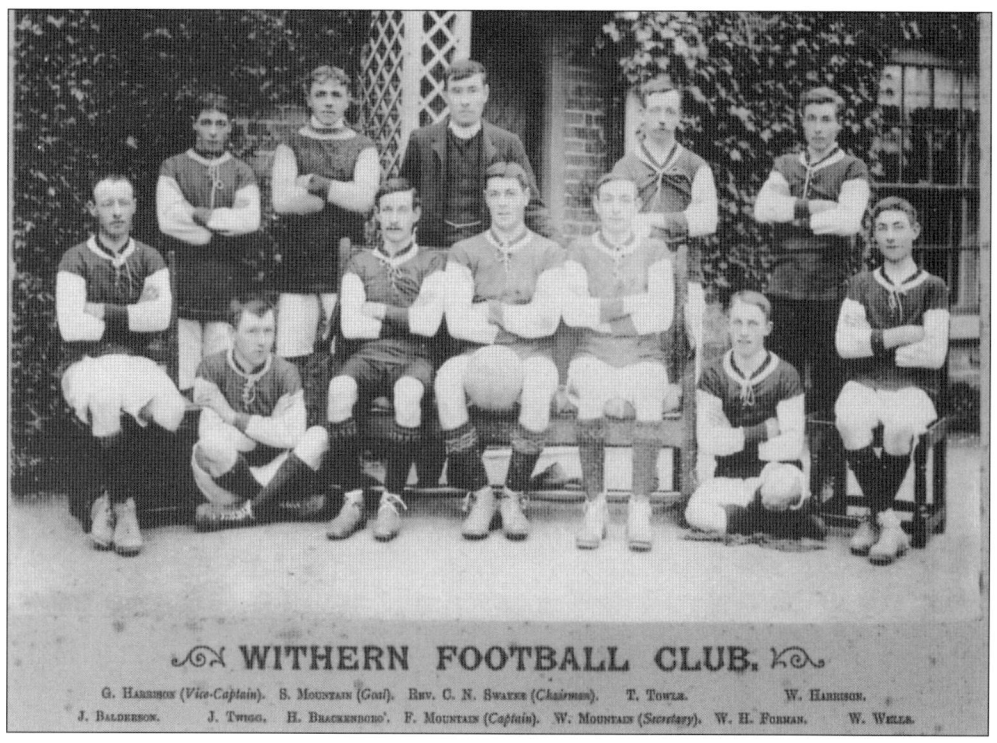

❧❧ WITHERN FOOTBALL CLUB. ❧❧

G. Harrison (*Vice-Captain*). S. Mountain (*Goal*). Rev. C. N. Swaine (*Chairman*). T. Towle. W. Harrison.

J. Balderson. J. Twigg. H. Brackenboro'. F. Mountain (*Captain*). W. Mountain (*Secretary*). W. H. Forman. W. Wells.

Withern football team, captain Fred Mountain, photographed at the Rectory c1910.

Withern Ladies' football team c1930.

generally, caused the committee to suspend operations. The death of JT Marshall in 1916 was a further blow and, in the dark days of 1917, it was decided to disband. The Society's net assets of £35-2s-6d were handed to the Red Cross and "a writing table was presented to Mr Slayton in recognition of his services as Hon. Secy."

During its life the Society attracted influential support. Patrons included:
- Lord Willoughby d'Eresby, MP;
- Viscount Alverstone, GCMG, appointed Lord Chief Justice in 1900;
- Sir Robert Perks, MP for Louth 1892-1906 [an early proponent of the Channel Tunnel];
- Canon Pretyman, of Great Carlton;
- Colonel CW Carr-Calthrop, son of the late Dr WC Calthrop of Withern [and brother of Lady Alverstone] (21); and
- Baroness von Eckardstein, heiress of the 'Maples' furniture store in London and builder of 'Petwood' at Woodhall Spa, who married Captain [later Sir Archibald] Weigall, MP for Horncastle 1911-20.

Among the Society's Presidents were Alderman JW Davy, Captain Weigall, MP, and TG Tickler, MP. Major Higgins, JP, was a Vice-President.

A major prize at the Shows, the 'Members' Spade', was awarded to John Beels [1910], Amos Bullivant [1911], and H Millson [1913]. Other prizewinners at the Shows included:

Cartwright & Pickering's Prize: H Paynter [1907], Tom Borman [1909], H Wilson, Aby [1911] and Tom Sivel [1913]

Toogood's Silver Shield: Charles Massey [1904, 1907, 1910 & 1913], Bill Bullivant [1908 & 1911], Amos Bullivant [1912] and C Broughton [1914]

Toogood's Bronze Medal: Bill Bullivant [1904, 1907, 1909, 1910, 1913 & 1914], John Beels [1905] and Charles Massey [1906]

The Cottage Garden 1st Prize: Tom Borman [1902, 1906 & 1910], John Beels [1903, 1905 & 1912], J Fawcett [1907 & 1911], PC Newman, Aby [1908], T Beels [1909] and Amos Bullivant [1914].

The Cartwright & Pickering Prize was a 'Perfect Washer'.

Allotments

The produce exhibited at the Show had to be grown somewhere and not everyone had a 'home close'. So, in 1894 one of the newly-formed Parish Council's first concerns was to provide allotments, for which the competition was considerable. The Council wanted Atkin's Field, a site of ten acres on the Alford Road, but the Steward of the Vyner Estate would not co-operate. In 1897 six acres were measured off in "*the field known as Woodhills adjoining the Alford Road*" for allotments at 35s-0d an acre, the first holders being Sam Sivel, Wright Watson, C Webster, G Clarke, Solomon Ashlin and John Watson.

Until 1918 there were also three sections of allotments off Gold Lane. When the Stovin Estate was sold, Fred Mountain, the purchaser of Laurels, was unwilling to continue the arrangement and the Parish Council had to find an alternative site. It eventually accepted three acres offered by James Pocklington, who had recently acquired Grange Farm.

Capt Brown with the Withern Scouts and Cubs c1930.

The Guide Captain, Mrs Perry, with a group of Withern Guides c1930.

Withern Brass Band

According to George Holmes, the Withern Brass Band was formed by the rector, Frederick Glover, using instruments left to him by an old lady. Glover, an accomplished musician with a music degree from Trinity College, Dublin, taught the bandsmen their notes and instructed them how to play; he also provided their uniforms. The band became one of the best in the district, playing for social functions for miles around under Bandmaster Edley Mountain. It performed regularly at the Withern Shows from 1901 to 1908, but it proved difficult to keep up public appearances. Although reported to have dissolved in 1909, the band seems to have appeared occasionally, for, in 1913, the Show Committee received a letter "*from Mr E Mountain stating that the Withern Band would be unable to fulfil engagement.*" The band ceased performing after the death of Edley Mountain in January 1914. It was revived in the 1930s, but the new band - Phil Blades, Amos Bullivant and Hal Holmes [saxhorns], Fred Mountain [bass saxhorn] and Edley White, Jack White and J Wright [cornets] - had a more modern military style of uniform.(22)

The Conservative Club

An active Conservative Association, formed in Withern before the Great War, largely through the influence of Dr and Mrs McNabb, had a hall in the village, a rather unsightly building, smaller than the present Village Hall, located where the house Haywain now stands. It was a centre of village social activity, based very much on the paternalist concern of the better-off sections of society for those dependent on them for employment. In the 'Workingmen's Conservative Club' in 1913 a typical village 'entertainment' comprised the following:

Programme

- pianoforte duet	the Misses Enderby
- song	Mr Swayne
- gramophone selection	
- play: 'The Backward Child'	Miss D Enderby and Miss L Fountain
- song	A Searby
- song	Mr H Watson
- song	Miss Tickler
- old English dance	Miss Hasnipp, Gayton-le-Marsh
- song	Mr Swayne
- gramophone selection	
- whistling solo	Miss D Enderby [encored]
- song	Dr McNabb
- play: 'Aunt Matilda's	Miss Payne, Misses Marshall, Miss Milson Children' [Aby], Miss Saul, Miss Tickler

Harry Watson, who sang a solo in this concert, was Dorothy Enderby's accompanist when she performed at local events.

Dr McNabb had been a medical officer on a ship before coming to Withern. He was a short man, with a white beard, renowned for calling on households at dinner-time when he would happily accept offers to eat with the family, saying: "*Oh, I might as well; my wife doesn't feed me!"* He and his formidable wife dominated village life for over forty years and 'their' Conservative Club provided regular dances until the 1960s. The Mayfair Accordion Band [Bill Bark and Syd and George Lowis] - in white shirts and red ties, with a shield displaying their emblem - played at these dances in the late 1930s. Mrs Al Searby and Mrs McNabb taught the youngsters to dance - and made sure they did, the young man observing all the old world courtesies when asking the young lady for a dance or seeing his partner back to her seat. If Mrs Searby and her partner chose to dance a polka, the other dancers would gradually drift away, leaving the floor to the expert pair, who would be watched with admiration as the music speeded up!

The Institute

The other centre of social life in the village, the 'Institute', was for many years the meeting place for the Women's Institute and the Withern Scouts. This small wooden building stood on the site of the garage at Glenmair. The Scouts later erected their own premises on the Alford Road.

The 'Club' and the 'Institute' were demolished in the 1960s. When the Scout troop folded a Village Hall Committee took over its building, which, much improved, is now the Withern Village Hall.

Football

Withern had a football team before the Great War. The chairman was the Rector, the Revd Noel Swayne, and the captain Fred Mountain sr. Fred was over six feet tall, a big, strong centre-forward, who at one stage received an offer to join Sheffield United. His brother Sid was the goalkeeper and a cousin, Will Mountain, played inside-left and served as the team's secretary. The vice-captain, George Harrison, was a grandson of Cook Harrison, the thrashing machine owner. Others in the team included George's brother Will, Tommy Towle [for many years sexton at St Margaret's Church], John Twigg, Wally Wells [from Brook Farm], and WH Forman.

After the Great War there were three teams in the village, players in the 1920s including Walter Barber and Edley White [goalkeepers], Harry Maddison [a carpenter from Strubby], Frank Burkitt and two Clark brothers. Sadly, over the years, interest waned and team football was eventually only played at the school. In the 1920s there was also a ladies' team. The pitches for both sports were in Crow Field behind Homeleigh; they were marked out with the powder residue from the carbide lighting system at the Rectory, which the young Joe Jesney and others collected on Saturday mornings. In Crow Field stood what Lol Patchett termed "*a chicken hut on wheels*", which served as a changing room; "*outside was a tin toilet.*"

Cricket

Local newspaper reports indicate that there was a cricket team in Withern in the 1880s, but little is known about it. After the Great War Withern had a cricket club running three teams. Frank Brown, JW [Joe] Perkins and Walter Swaby served as officers; EA [Ted] Millson was captain of the first team and Bert Mason vice-captain. Among the many players were Syd Ailsby, the Bosworths, George ['Daddy'] Clark, Walter Cox, Alan Dennis, John Drakes, Syd Harrison, Joe Jesney, Sid Lowis, Charlie Marshall, George Marwood, Bill and 'Ebor' Mason, Arthur and Bill Thorndike, Frank Watson and Edley White - to name but a few. Boys who longed to make the team included Roy Harrison, J Millson, John Mountain and Charlie Westerby. Basil Drakes and Ted Millson, two of the best all-round sportsmen in the district, were also good at soccer, cricket, shooting and ice-skating.

Cricket was revived in 1948 by Fred Mountain jr, Withern's answer to Denis Compton, and a band of enthusiasts at a public meeting held in the Village Institute. Fred was elected captain of the team and Roy Harrison vice-captain. Other leading members of the Withern & District Cricket Club during the next decade included Jim Elliott, Roy Jacklin, Frank Marshall [who lodged at Flaxmill Cottages], Jon Vinter, John Brookes, Eric Pocock [a very fast bowler], Wally White [son of Edley] and Arthur Westerby. In January 1959 'the first Annual Dinner' was held at the Red Lion at 10s-0d [50p] a ticket!

The excitement must have been great when Marshall scored 21 runs and took 5 wickets for 6 runs to trounce South Ormsby in June 1950, and again when Mountain scored 38 not out and took 4 wickets for 15 to give Withern victory over an Ellis & Thompson team. The following teams, taken from the score books, give an idea of those who played for Withern:

v RAF Strubby	v South Ormsby	v Mablethorpe
1948	**1950**	**1960**
F Marshall	G Cragg	F Mountain
G Anderson	G White	W White
A Westerby	J Mason	G Turner
F Mountain	F Marshall	G Parker
J Mountain	G Hoyles	D Pritchett
F Perry	F Mountain	H Westerby
R Harrison	D Wattam	J Hotchkin
J Mason	E Pocock	J Dawson
G Mawer	H Bullivant	M Sleaford
E Pocock	D Cox	R Harrison
R Jacklin	D Pocklington	M Vickers

In the 1960 season the Cricket Club's officers were:
Revd GR Bickerton, President
AE Frankum, Chairman
Mrs C Vinter, Treasurer
FE Mountain, Secretary and Captain
R Harrison, Vice-Captain.

Subscriptions were Seniors 10 shillings and Juniors 5 shillings. Opposition was provided by teams from Alford & District, Burgh, Grimoldby, Mablethorpe, North Somercotes and South Somercotes, as well as from organizations such as the County Infirmary, Fenland Laundry and the Rural District Council.

Although not generally very successful, the team provided great entertainment; members were driven to away matches by Joe Perkins in his taxi. (23)

Ice Skating and Ice Hockey

At the beginning of World War II the river between Withern Bridge and the mill pool was straightened. Previously a section of the field on the Withern side of the

Conservative Club Dance; Mrs McNabb, with walking stick, is sitting in the front row.

Withern WI outing to Bath in the early 1950s; the group includes Mrs Stratton, the rector's wife, in the front row.

river flooded and, in the cold winters of the time, conditions were ideal for ice skating and ice hockey; matches were played against Alford and Spilsby teams. Skates were often improvised blades screwed into the skater's boots. Among those who skated were Ted Millson, Jack Willmer and several lady schoolteachers.

Darts

Weekly darts tournaments were run by the British Legion for several winters in the 1940s. The Red Lion also had three teams in the Mablethorpe Darts League.

Car Rallying

In the 1950s Alan Burkitt raced motorcycles at Cadwell Park, a sport later taken up by John Brookes. With Dr Lord, Alan was also a regular participant in car rallies. Dr Lord is remembered for taking his Mini Cooper S with him when he made a lecture tour of the USA and Alaska.

Withern Women's Institute

The Withern branch of the Lindsey Federation of Women's Institutes was formed in 1925. So energetic was it that, within three years, under its President, Mrs W Swaby, it succeeded, at an exhibition in Scunthorpe, in beating 37 other branches to win the coveted County Banner, previously held by the Aby branch, and the County Produce Cup. The branch then had 40-50 members. The Vice-President was Mrs CE Searby, the Hon. Treasurer Mrs JW Pocklington, and the Hon. Secretary Miss A Carrott. The monthly meetings featured demonstrations [Mrs Jesney of Strubby did 'Trussing a fowl'], entertainment sketches and competitions.

Members took part in many WI activities across the county, including 'A Pageant of Lindsey', presented by the Lindsey Women's Institutes at Bayons Manor in June 1939. This comprised episodes in the history of England. Withern and other branches took part in the episode representing the 19th century, entitled 'The Good Old Times'; the programme described it as "*a Lady of the Manor dispensing gifts to the villagers*" and "*Foresters leading the annual procession to the Whitsun Fair.*"

Membership had dropped to around 30 by the mid-1950s, when Mrs Perkins was President and Mrs Laura Bullivant Secretary. The branch, which met in the Chapel school-room after the demise of the 'Institute', survived until the 1970s.

Flower Shows

In 1948 the local sub-branch of the British Legion revived the annual Withern Fruit, Flower and Vegetable Shows, one of those responsible being Walter Swaby. For some years after World War II the branch organized a twice-yearly show, which raised money to provide an outing and a Christmas present for each old person in the parish. The 5th British Legion Show, in 1952, had 400 exhibits, as well as sideshows and other attractions. The Swaby Prize for the exhibitor with the most points was awarded to Mr and Mrs W Spence; class winners included Mrs L Blackburn, JW Bullivant, G Clark, Mrs A Perry, T Mawer, CW Thorndike and Mrs E White.

In 1965 the show, then held in the Conservative Club and the adjoining field, was taken over by the Scouts and Guides. The British Legion Trophy for the vegetable section [still awarded each year] was presented in 1966 to Mr G Clark of Strubby, the flower trophy to Mrs Turner of Gayton-le-Marsh, and the cookery trophy jointly to Mrs

The Village Institute, which stood next to Glenmair and the Post Office [right].

Withern Players: the first pantomime - "Mother Goose" It proved so popular that an extra performance had to be arranged. Pictured are [left to right]: David Vinter, Shirley Watson, Joan Harrison, Ann Carr, Pearl Harrison, Richard Warne, Bill Bullivant, Joyce Jackson and, in front, Eddie Hall.

Marshall and Mrs Stratford. More than £95-0-0 were raised for the Scout Hut funds. Dr Robert McNabb came from Watford to open the 1974 Show.

In recent years the show has been an annual event run by the Village Hall Committee.

Pantomimes

The Withern pantomimes, such as 'Aladdin' and 'Mother Goose', produced by the Revd GR Bickerton, were staged in the School or the Conservative Club in the 1950s and 60s. All ages took part in these 'Withern Dramatic Society' productions, players including Chris and Deborah Bickerton, Bill Bullivant, John Brookes, Ann Carr, Anne Dunham, Joan and Pearl Harrison, David Vinter, Richard Warne, Shirley Watson, Ann Westerby and others. Younger participants included Peter Bullivant, Margaret Ingram, Pam Shepherd and Rachel Vinter. Bennett Maltson played the piano and Tom Sempers, a local electrician, managed the scenery.

In 1968 the Withern Players performed two one-act plays - 'Not What They Seem' and 'Goose Chase' - produced by Mrs Shepherd, the programme including a comedy duet and Alastair Stones, with his electric guitar, singing songs and leading community singing.

WITHERN
METHODIST CHURCH

SUNDAY, SEPTEMBER 26th, 1971

ANNUAL

HARVEST
THANKSGIVING
SERVICES

conducted by the newly appointed
Superintendent Minister

REV. JOHN NEWTON

2.30 p.m.   Children's Gift Service
6.00 p.m.   Thanksgiving Service

Organist: MR. GEORGE ALVEY of Mablethorpe
Soloist: MRS. OLIVE WILLSON of Trusthorpe

Gifts of fruit, vegetables, etc., for decoration of the
Chapel will be gratefully received

Chapter 14:
The Parish 1920-75

The last chapter of the Withern story finishes with the closing of the church and the centenary of the chapel. Inevitably, space only permits a few of the events of the years 1920-75 to be included.

Between the Wars

After the Great War life in the village changed. The end of the old estates was probably viewed with mixed feelings, as both had provided stability and looked after their properties. The freeholder farmers who succeeded them did not offer the care previously shown and, as one villager remarked: "*Life was never the same after the sale*."

In January 1920 the Parish Council held an Extraordinary Meeting to consider a letter received from the Chairman of the War Agricultural Committee about the extermination of rats. It was decided to offer 3d for each rat killed in the parish on the production of the tail; six weeks later the Clerk reported that he "*had received 198 rats' tails, amounting to £2-9s-6d*". The offer continued into the summer.

New people arrived, but villagers continued to move away. Some went to the towns and some emigrated. The population, 407 in 1911, gradually declined to a low point of 296 in 1961, a reduction of 27% in fifty years. In the 1920s Chattertons acquired the smithy and Edwin Lowis the carpenter's shop. In the 1930s, when the carpentry business ended, CD Pocklington acquired the old Three Tuns Inn, where he developed the bakery, which became a major business in the area.

Alf Frankum, who had come to Withern as chauffeur to Dr McNabb, recalled the village before the Great War having had "*a blacksmith's shop with two or three men working there, a carpenter's shop with two or three men, and a butcher*." By the 1960s all had disappeared.

The War Memorial

A war memorial, commemorating those who died on military service during the Great War, was erected to the north of the almshouses in 1921, the site being conveyed that summer by Lady Mary Compton-Vyner to Arthur Enderby and Fred Searby, 'Trustees of the Withern War Memorial Committee'. These trustees died in the 1940s and for some years the memorial was maintained by the Withern Sub-branch of the British Legion. When the branch ceased to exist the Parish Council assumed the responsibility.

The Red Lion

After the death of JT Marshall, Dick Staines became the licensee and farmer at the Red Lion. One possibly jaundiced observer has remarked that he wanted the farm, not the pub, and served beer through a window rather than allow people inside! In those days there was a sheep dip behind the pub. By the 1920s Charles Berry had taken over. He was followed by Frank Willmer, who died in 1929. John Alfred Pocock, the next landlord, was succeeded in 1954 by his son-in-law, Don Twidale.

Temperance

The Revd James Holden, a popular Vicar of Strubby 1916-30, worked hard for the cause of temperance, an important feature of local life between the wars. The Rechabite's 'Ebenezer Tent' [No. 4103] in Withern, which may have been dormant, had been re-formed in 1912. Joe Perkins was the Secretary in 1923 when the Tent had 28 members and held meetings in the Chapel schoolroom [the juvenile section's Dreadnought Tent had 4 members]. In the late 1920s the Tent met at George Harrison's house. The Methodists, who had embraced teetotalism in the 1870s, had many members active in both the Band of Hope and the Rechabites in the 1920s and 30s.

Motor Vehicles

In Peters Lane Mrs Clark, in her bonnet, was still operating as a horse and cart carrier to Louth [she charged 3d each to bring parcels from Louth], but the advent of motor vehicles began to make life less peaceful. The motors were, of course, a far cry from modern vehicles, a memorable sight being the Brooke Bond van - a Trojan - red, with no side windows, and chain driven. The salesmen wore pinstripes and bowler hats.

By 1928 the amount of traffic highlighted the need for Main Road to be widened at the junction with the Alford Road ['Enderby's Corner']. The roadworks led to a Royal Enfield motorcycle combination overturning on loose material left at the bend. PC West and Dr McNabb assisted the driver to Chatterton's smithy where his injuries were treated. He was then taken by car back to friends in Mablethorpe. It is probably unkind to see the driver, a visiting Yorkshireman, as an early example of a speeding tourist.

'Withern Aerodrome'

In the 1930s a fascinating sight for local boys was Alex Henshaw, the famous aviator from Sutton-on-Sea, flying from Withern Bottom [near the river at Barfen]. Alex was looking for a new base for his flying activities, when, in 1934, Eric West, the farmer at Barfen, allowed him to use one of his fields and to relocate his aircraft hangar from Skegness. In 1935 Alex, who had been flying a Leopard Moth with limited success, bought a single seater Arrow Active metal biplane, powered by a Cirrus Hermes IIB engine. He flew the Active from Withern, but, sadly, at the end of the year its engine exploded during a flight and the plane crashed in a field near Covenham; Alex jumped out of the burning plane and survived, thanks to his parachute. During 1936, using the Leopard, he won the London to Isle of Man Race and the Contact Race at Birmingham. In his next plane, a Percival Mew Gull [G-AEXF], Alex won the King's Cup in 1938 and broke all England-Capetown-England records in a spectacular manner in 1939. But by then Barfen's short-lived days as 'Withern Aerodrome' had ceased; he had moved his home airfield to Hagnaby in 1937. His fame as an aviator continued into World War II, when, as Supermarine's chief test pilot, he flew probably 10% of all the Spitfires ever built.

Perkins' shop and garage c1920.

The blacksmiths at the Forge c1920.

Withern Silver Jubilee Celebrations, May 6th, 1935.

The Silver Jubilee of King George V

In 1935 Withern celebrated the King's Silver Jubilee in style. There was a large committee, the officers being:

> Chairman: Dr AAJ McNabb
> Vice-Chairman: the Revd WC Perry
> Secretaries: Captain F Brown and Captain W Swaby
> Treasurer: JW Perkins.

They spent several months raising funds for a "*fitting celebration*", producing £65, a great sum for those days. On the day there were flags, bunting and streamers through the entire length of the village. A service in St Margaret's Church was conducted by the Rector; the Withern Scouts [Scoutmaster: Capt. Brown] and Guides [Captain: Mrs Perry] were present and the organ was played by the local teacher, Freddie Ladds. The Rector had sent a message of congratulation to the King and Queen on behalf of the parish and read out the reply he had received from the King's Private Secretary. Specially prepared boxes were sent by the committee to all those unable to attend the festivities due to illness or infirmity.

In the afternoon there was a fancy dress parade and races were held for the children. Lol Patchett came 2nd in the 25 yards flat race for under 7s, A and F Westerby were 2nd in the three-legged race for under 10s, and M Berry won the 100 yards for girls aged 10-14. Later the children had tea in a large marquee. On leaving the tea-table each child was presented with a souvenir mug by Mrs McNabb and a Jubilee medal by Mrs Perry. Further races took place while the adults had tea. In the evening the adults had a fancy dress parade, won by Mrs Perkins jr ['Grandma Buggins'], and sports events - the mixed wheelbarrow race was won by Mr and Mrs C Searby, Miss V Farrow came 3rd in the ladies' 80 yards flat race, and W Thorndike's team beat T Lowe's team in the final of the tug of war.

During the evening two 20ft 'fire balloons' were released by Messrs E White and A Frankum. The climax of the evening was when the Scouts were gathered with lighted torches and paraded round the sports field and thence to the adjoining field where "a huge bonfire over 20ft in height and 40 yards in circumference had been specially built by E White, J Perkins, R Sivel, A Frankum, J Perkins jr, R Mason, A Searby, W Thorndike and many other willing helpers". In making the fire they used 20 loads of faggots and thorns and a large quantity of waste material, about 100 old motor tyres and a quantity of tar and paraffin! When the Alford beacon was seen to have been lit, a rocket was fired and the Scouts lit the fire, which blazed for hours. The finale was "*a grand display of Brock's special Jubilee fireworks*".

Thrashing Machines

Harrisons' thrashing machine business continued until George Harrison sr died in 1929, when the business was sold.(24)

George Vamplew, who lived at Homeleigh, also had a thrashing machine business in Withern for some years and there was a little rivalry between the two concerns, Harrisons with their dull, well-worn machines and Vamplew with his polished machines, their brass parts shining. Vamplew kept his machines at the yard behind Wilson's Cottage [Karatangi]. After he moved to Authorpe the yard became known as 'Syd Anderson's yard'. Syd was well-known for his skill with a gun and his ability to shoot game.

The death of Bill Bullivant

Shortly before World War II one of old Withern's leading figures died. Bill Bullivant's ancestors had been tenants of the lords of the manor of Withern for about 200 years before purchasing Home Farm in 1920 [his father, another William, had moved there in the 1860s]. Bill, a trustee of the Withern Court of the Foresters and player of the big bass drum in the Withern Band before the Great War, had been a keen gardener, winning 77 prizes at the Withern Show in 1913, including 19 firsts and 19 seconds. His wife Mary was a daughter of James Clark, the carrier.

Home Farm and Hillcrest, the homes of Bill and Amos Bullivant, which had been old thatched farmhouses, were rebuilt in the late 1930s.

World War II 1939-45

Before World War II, when work was not easy to find, some local men emigrated and some joined up, holding the view that war was inevitable. Bill Clark, George's brother, and Walter Cox were among the volunteers; Great War veterans also rejoined the colours, among them Walter Swaby, Bert Patchett and Charlie Watson. Among the many stories told about the war days are the following.

Bomber Crash:

There was great excitement one night in 1940 when a Handley Page 'Hampden' bomber of 144 Squadron, on its way back to RAF Hemswell from a sortie over Germany, ran out of fuel and crash-landed at Withern Bottom. The crew - PO Hartop, Sgt Kirby, Sgt Burns and Sgt Daniels - survived the experience and walked to Brook Farm where Willows Farrow gave assistance.

When another bomber crash-landed in Withern in September 1944 - this time a Halifax, type III, number MZ 758, returning from operations over Venlo in Holland - the reception was less friendly. The plane, which was heading for RAF Snaith in Yorkshire, had engine trouble and the pilot received permission to land at RAF Strubby. Heading inland from the coast, he was unable to complete a turning manoeuvre in the direction of Strubby. After trimming the hedge from Barfen to Withern with a wing, the plane flopped down in a field of peas between the Highland Drain and the river to the west of Calf Fen Lane [the field, behind Willows Farm/Fairview, was owned by Fred Mountain]. The pilot and crew - W/O Potts, F/Sgt Frew, the navigator, F/Sgt Hobbs, the bomb aimer, F/Sgt Patey, the wireless operator, Sgt McGowan, the flight engineer, Sgt Howard, the MU gunner, and Sgt Hale, the rear gunner - managed to leave the plane, used one of the bomb doors to bridge the Highland Drain, and walked across the fields to Main Road. The first farmer they called on thought they were Germans and phoned the Police! The men trudged on to another farm where they were looked after. It had been a close shave. One of those responsible for removing the aircraft told a survivor that the wing of the plane had missed a tree in the hedge by only a few feet; if the wing had hit the tree, the plane would have catapulted and all the crew would probably have been killed.

Stain's mock airfield:

Sam Stones recalled a mock airfield being constructed at Stain to serve as a decoy for enemy aircraft; as a result Stain was bombed!

Bombs: Strubby, too, was bombed, one landing on the green lane running up to the airfield from Strubby New Town.

106

Withern Aerodrome: Alex Henshaw with his Arrow Active, a metal bi-plane, at Barfen, December 1935. [Reproduced by permission of Mr Alex Henshaw]

Withern Home Guard during World War II; among their duties was the guarding of local road bridges at night.

Rockets:

Early in the war [c1941] rockets were test fired in the field on the Aby side of Withern Wood. About 4 feet long and 3 inches in diameter, they were prototypes for a means of foiling enemy aircraft by releasing silver paper into the air [this would damage propellors, fuselage, etc]. They produced small parachutes to lessen the impact when they landed. Some of the Withern Home Guard watched the site being set up. When the rockets were fired, the darkness and wartime 'blackout' made it impossible for locals to see where the rockets went. Some dropped on faggot heaps in Mr Thorndike's yard at Three Acres. It was then decided that Withern was an unsuitable location for potentially dangerous tests and the project was transferred to Acre Gap at Sutton-on-Sea.

The Blacker Bombard:

A gun emplacement was constructed on the south-east corner of 'Castle Hill'. An ash tree was felled and the trunk placed upright in a hole dug in the mound; four legs and an iron bar placed through the top of the tree trunk kept the gun stable. The gun, a Blacker Bombard, was an almost suicidal weapon intended to combat invasion of the Lindsey coast. This 29mm Spigot Mortar, invented by a Lieutenant-Colonel Blacker in the early years of the war as a cheap replacement for ordnance lost at Dunkirk, was very heavy (around 350lbs) and, with its 4 legged portable mounting, was said to need a crew of 6 to move it. It fired a 20lb fin-stabilized anti-tank bomb warhead containing a high explosive charge and had the drawback that, when the warhead hit its target, the fins had a habit of flying backwards along the original trajectory and endangering the firing crew - its effective range with the anti-tank bomb was around 100-150 yards, so the firing crew was expected to wait until any tanks were at close range! It was also capable of firing a 14 lb anti-personnel bomb with a maximum range of around 500 yards. Rejected by the regular army, the Blacker Bombard was used by the Home Guard and airfield protection units in 1941-44. In Withern's case the gun was only fired once - when tested at Partney - and was considered dangerous by those who manned it.

Withern Fire Brigade:

The wartime Withern 'fire brigade' kept its fire engine in a trap-house at Manor Farm for a while when the Perkins family lived there. The old well in Pocklington's field, which still existed on the site of Vear's farm, was used for testing the pump engine.

The Home Guard:

Shortly after the declaration of a state of war, Ernie Ingram was approached by the authorities and deputed to form a local group of 'parashots', whose role was to attack parachute invaders by shooting [he was sent a rifle and some rounds of ammunition, but no uniform]. Together with George Lowis and Cyril Pocklington, who had already volunteered for war service, he started the forerunner of Withern's Local Defence Volunteers [created in May 1940 and later renamed the Home Guard]. One of the Home Guard's duties was to place sentries on the Withern and Stain bridges around sunrise and sunset.

Civil Defence:

On Main Road an old outbuilding of the Red Lion, which stood behind a brick wall on the site of the school car park, was designated a 'Cleaning Station'. In the event of a gas attack, people were to be 'cleansed' there; fortunately, it never served its purpose.

Killed in Action:

The parish lost two young men on active service:

- Charlie Westerby, son of Eva and Ernest Westerby, who lived between the village centre shops, was killed near Brussels in 1944; and
- Fred Searby, son of Albert Searby of Willows and nephew of Fred Searby, the War Memorial trustee, was killed in Italy.

Those who stayed at home also played their part through Civil Defence and the Home Guard or by working in agriculture - feeding the nation was an important part of the war effort. JW 'Young Bill' Bullivant was Chief Air Raid Warden, just one of the many roles he played in Withern life - he was also a churchwarden for many years, a parish councillor, an almshouse trustee and a pantomime artist.

RAF Strubby

With the impact it had on Withern [a tiny section of it being in Withern parish], it is appropriate to mention the airfield at Strubby. Built for Bomber Command in 1943, it was first used by Coastal Command for attacking German E Boats off the Dutch coast. Lancasters of Bomber Command's 619 and 227 Squadrons arrived in the autumn of 1944 and by April 1945 the station strength was about 1,450. Bomber Command departed in July 1945 and the station became, for a while, home to four maintenance units preparing for service in the Far East. After the war the airfield was integrated with and used by the RAF Flying College at Manby; Vampires, Hunters, Canberras and Meteors were among the many aircraft which flew regularly out of Strubby in the next twenty years. In 1953 it served as temporary quarters for 400 soldiers drafted in to help rebuild the sea defences after the East Coast floods. The station closed in 1972.

After The War

After the upheaval of the war years, the peace was soon shattered for the people of Withern by the tragic killing of a newly born baby at Saul's Cottage [a house which formerly stood at Longlands] on a winter evening in 1945. A young tractor driver was subsequently convicted and imprisoned for murder.

The shock of this event was followed by the blizzards of late January to early March 1947. Temperatures plummeted; 30° of frost and several feet of snow made life almost impossible across the country. A little late, perhaps, the mains electricity supply came into service in Withern in January 1948. Those who had been relying on oil lamps and candles for lighting and oil stoves and coal fires for heating must have been delighted. A few more fortunate people, such as the Rector, had had generators to provide a little electricity for lighting.

In 1948, with Lindsey County Council approval, three seats - at Manor Farm corner, Peters Lane corner, and the War Memorial - were erected by the Parish Council with money from the 'Homecoming Fund' in memory of the two men who had been killed in World War II. In 1965 the Parish Council accepted an offer by Mr Gledhill to provide a seat near the Wells Close bungalows.

Shops
The Supply Stores [Post Office]:

Walter Swaby, who arrived in 1920, had the telephone number Withern 1. As well as being postmaster, he sold groceries, paraffin, boots, shoes, sweets and cigarettes and measured people for clothes. Swaby's precise ways did not always endear him to children. Grace Wright preferred to go to Mr Perkins' shop to get her sweets - "We didn't go to Mr Swaby as he used to weigh them out, but Perkins screwed up a cone of newspaper and put plenty of sweets in." Syd Lowis was the Swaby errand boy in the early 1930s. The shop closed when Capt. Swaby rejoined the Army in World War II [he became Quartermaster for the Home Guard in Alford] and Joe Perkins took over the grocery delivery rounds. The Supply Stores and Post Office reopened after the war.

'Captain' Swaby was a rather snobbish man. Gerry Abbott, who lived in the School House and taught at Alford Secondary Modern School, was greeted by him in the Post Office one morning: "Good morning, Abbott. You were in the Army during the war. Would you like to join the British Legion? What rank did you achieve - Sergeant?" Abbott replied: "*No. Actually I was a Major.*" Swaby never mentioned the army or the war again.

When Walter Swaby retired, the shop was acquired by the Lazenby family, who were followed, in turn, by Cookes, Trewecks and Peirsons.

The Village Stores:

Fred 'Twinnie' Jackson ran this shop until his death in 1942, selling all kinds of goods, including groceries, boots and cheap plimsolls, which were worn by the children of poor families in the summer. The shop again served as the village post office during World War II. When Fred died in 1942 the shop was run for a while by his widow, with their daughter Grace running the post office. It was then taken over by the Hoyles family, who were followed by the Hills and the Gledhills.

Perkins:

Joe Perkins expanded his business after he moved it along the road. From bicycles he graduated to cars and developed a garage-cum-service station, as well as the shop, on the new site. Here were sold groceries, sweets, cigarettes, wellington boots, paraffin, etc. Another service to local cottagers was the collection of eggs, butter and poultry, which were taken to Stennett's Wednesday market in Louth. Grocery deliveries covered Mablethorpe, Trusthorpe and Sutton-on-Sea, as well as villages as far away as Cumberworth. The shop, which had its own generator to provide electricity, also supplied power for the lights in the neighbouring Chapel. Ernie Ingram, who had come to Withern in 1938 to work at the newly created trout farm at Withern Mill, took over the business, then in a corrugated iron building, in 1945. The Ingrams ran the business for 29 years, retiring in 1974.

Frankums:

Alf [AE] Frankum, who came from Reading to be chauffeur to Dr McNabb, lost his job some time after being invalided out of the Army; he had been in the Boer War and was a Sergeant in the Seaforth Highlanders during the Great War. To earn a living he started a round selling fish in 1921. Each morning at about 5.00 a.m. he drove his pony and cart to Aby Station to meet the Grimsby train. He would buy a box of iced fish, take it home and sort it, and then set off round the villages in the district selling it. His best customers were not in Withern, where his main sales occurred at the end of the day when he made a second round selling, more cheaply, the fish he had left! He began to sell other items, such as salt and pepper [to go with the fish] and groceries, gradually building up a grocery round; in 1925 he acquired a Model T Ford.

The family lived in Gledhill Drive and rented from the Post Office the buildings at the rear of Fred Jackson's shop - a stable, with two big doors, and a shed in which they stored their goods, vans etc. His son, also Alf [1907-62], who learnt to drive in 1922, joined the business and by 1929 the family had acquired a van [the first Bedford-built Chevrolet van], which they kept until 1936.

Alf junior built a new shop on Main Road in 1951 and, in 1953, his son Bob returned to the business after National Service. In 1954, when rationing ended, Frankums joined several other local traders in buying direct from manufacturers. This enabled the local shops to compete on price with the larger chains of grocery stores – an early example of the power of bulk purchasing. A new Bedford van was bought in 1955 to serve as a mobile shop, this being replaced later by a tailor-made mobile shop. Although Bob Frankum moved to a shop at Grimoldby in 1968, he ran the mobile shop in Withern for a few more years and his mother, Mrs Suie Frankum, traded at the Main Road shop until her retirement in 1980, selling, as she told the local newspaper, *"hardware and food of all sorts, towels, wellingtons, string, cigarettes and sweets."*

The property was then sold; the shop was eventually acquired by the local medical practice and converted into a surgery. The decaying cottage next to the shop, which had originally been mud and stud with a thatched roof [the walls had been bricked over and tiles placed on the thatch], was demolished after the departure of the Frankums. A reminder of old Withern, this building was probably known to the Gresswells in the 18th century.

Surgery

For many years the doctor's surgery was at Woodlands in Chalk Lane [the 'Doctor's House']. Old Dr McNabb died at the beginning of World War II. He had been joined in the Withern practice by his son, Dr Robert McNabb, who qualified in medicine in the 1930s. When Robert later entered into a partnership with Dr Temple and others in Alford, the surgery continued in a building at Woodlands, where old Mrs McNabb still lived. Robert McNabb later moved south to further his medical career and the Alford partnership built a new doctor's house and surgery in Church Lane [Great Heck]. Dr 'Jack' Lord, one of the partners, operated from this house in the 1950s.(25) Great Heck was sold c1962 and a new surgery opened in a building at the rear of the village Post Office, where it remained until c1985 when new owners of the Post Office, unhappy with its presence, refused to renew the arrangement. It was then decided to develop a surgery on the site of Frankum's shop.(25)

Social Life

In the years after the war, before television established its hold on society, there was a lot of social activity in Withern. Anglicans and Methodists worked together and supported each other's events. There were many groups in the village, such as the Women's Institute, the Young Wives, the British Legion, the Withern Scouts and Guides [and Cubs and Brownies], the Mid-Marsh Travelling Guild, the Wednesday Club, the Withern Players, the Evergreen Club and the Forget-Me-Not Club.

The miserable weather at the time of the Coronation of Queen Elizabeth II in 1953 upset Withern's celebrations, described by the Standard as *"one of the most ambitious programmes"* in the district. But one event was not delayed - the presentation of a souvenir mug to each child.

By contrast, a beautiful Saturday afternoon in the summer of 1959 helped the Garden Fete held by Mrs Stovin at Aby Grange to raise nearly £200 towards improvements to the Withern Almshouses. There was a dance in the Conservative Club in the evening. Social and charitable events were regular features of life in the parish.

The almshouses were again the beneficiaries in December 1967, when a coffee party organized by Dr Lord and Mrs Vinter raised £44-0-0. On the same day the Over 65s went to the Playgoers in Louth to see the latest production - 'Job for a Boy'. The following week Christmas parcels were taken to 76 people in the village by the Evergreen Club and plum bread was delivered to the over 65s of the village by members of the British Legion. In between, the church, the chapel, the school and the Scouts all had carol services, a bring and buy sale took place at the school, a games night was held in the newly erected Scout Hall, and there was an outing for the over 60s to a Louth pantomime – 'Babes in the Wood'.

It was in 1967 that the 1st Withern Scout Troop received the Chittenden Trophy for the most proficient troop in the district and five of the Venture Scouts passed their examination for the Fireman Badge at Mablethorpe Fire Station.

While blizzards brought the whole district to a standstill in 1968, a happier event occurred when Edley White, land drainage supervisor with the Alford Internal Drainage Board, who lived opposite The Laurels, was awarded the British Empire Medal for his services to the Board and its predecessors since 1936.

Church and Chapel
The Church:

Samuel Frost, who succeeded Noel Swayne in 1919, and Robert Norwood, in 1922, were the last Rectors presented by a Vyner.

Although 73 years old when he arrived, William Corbett Perry, who succeeded Norwood in 1927, was able and effective. The last 'grand' Victorian rector, he was the son of George Perry, Ironmaster at the Mitre Works in Darlaston, Staffordshire, and had been Head Master of Queen Elizabeth School, Worcester, before becoming a full-time priest in 1898. Mrs Perry ran the Withern Guides.

The next rector, Ethelbert Vaughan [1936-38], a reserved High Churchman in his sixties who had served many years in India and the West Indies, wore a 'skullcap'. From this time the influence of the Church began an irreversible decline.

Although nearly 70 years old and disabled, William Howe [1938-46], who succeeded Vaughan, was an approachable, well respected man and a talented artist. He was buried at Withern, as were his daughter [1956] and widow [1966].

Samuel Stratton [1946-55], who entered the Church in his forties, was Vicar of Strubby [1931-55] before coming to Withern. A kindly, quiet man, he had a friendly and well-liked wife, who dispensed cod liver oil and orange juice at the Rectory in the 1940s when Red Cross baby clinics were to be found in most villages.

Geoffrey Bickerton, rector 1955-66, was a jovial, friendly man, who formed a church choir and the village dramatic society which produced the very popular pantomimes; many villagers, young and old, took part. He died in Kirkcaldy, Scotland, in 1972. While in Withern Mrs Bickerton was an active Rural District councillor.

Ernest Pitman, a Canon of Qu'Appelle, Saskatchewan, in the Province of Rupert's Land, Canada, was rector 1967-71. Already in his sixties, and with his wife often in hospital, he was seen by some as having assisted the moves to close the church.

The last rector to hold the living was Neil Strong [1971-75], a serious Evangelical with a commitment to the ecumenical movement. He fostered closer co-operation between the Anglican and Methodist Churches in Withern and South Reston and joint use of the Methodist Chapels. When George Parrott, priest-in-charge 1975-90, succeeded him the two parish churches were no longer used and the amalgamation of livings was well under way.

The Methodist Chapel:

While the Church declined, the Chapel continued to be a popular centre of religious worship. The 'new' Chapel celebrated its 50th anniversary in June 1925 with special services and "*A Sacred Concert by Alford Wesleyan Choir*". A "*Great Public Meeting*" [chairman Mrs Wintringham JP] was addressed by the Revd Thomas Naylor, Chairman of the District, and by Methodist Circuit Ministers; there was also a special soloist, Miss Nancy Jewell.

A Sale of Work in 1929 raised £30-15s-4$\frac{1}{2}$d and a Garden Party the following year £30-17s-8d. Much of the unusually high income was spent on refurbishing the Chapel. A Fête was held in 1931 and several Garden Parties in 1937-42, but from 1943 an annual Gift Day and the Harvest Festival became the main sources of revenue. A sign of the changing times was the decline in giving. Less money was produced by most of the Gift Days in the late 1960s than by those in the 1940s and 50s. Only with the inflation of the 1970s did income from Gift Days show a significant increase.

Improvements were made in 1948 when H Kirby of Louth was paid £335-6s-11d for installing 200ft of tubular heating and four convector fires in the building. At the Switching-On ceremony a number of switches were operated by invited guests, including Mrs Burkitt of Withern.

The Chapel celebrated its 75th Anniversary on 25 June 1950 and its centenary celebrations on 13 July 1975, when an exhibition was staged illustrating the life of the Church and the community during the previous 160 years; there were floral decorations, a produce stall, and a joint Methodist/Church of England family service led by the Revd George Parrott.

Death of Two Well-known Methodists:

Two well-known Methodists died in 1974. Fred Mountain, captain of the Withern football team before the Great War, was 86. Born at Rose Cottage, he had farmed at Laurels since 1919, when he bought the farm from the old Stovin estate.

Another life-long resident, Charles Marwood, was 90. Born in Eight House Row into a family of twelve, he had spent his working life at Red Lion Farm and lived in the adjoining white house. He had been a regular prizewinner at the Withern Shows, and a member of the Foresters' Court Good Intent and latterly of the Alford Court.

Laurels Farm: Fred Mountain and his daughter Rose watching cows leave the cow shed at Laurels in 1952 when cattle were driven regularly along Main Road to pasture near Home Farm. Cattle meal and Mrs Mountain's fowls were kept in the shed at the rear. The low building between the sheds was the milk-cooling parlour. The Mountains sold the farm in 1977. 'The Laurels' is now a house; a bungalow, 'The Old Well', stands on the site of the buildings in the picture.

The Arrival of Modern Services

The mains water supply arrived in Withern in the 1950s – a major advance, water having previously been taken from wells and, at Withern Hall, by a ram at the river at Withern Mill. In the late 1960s sewerage and housing became important issues in Withern. At the larger houses sewage was passed into cesspits, which drained into the dykes, but the smaller homes had to put up with the 'night-soil' cart coming to empty their back yard privies. The Rural District Councillor [Mrs Bickerton] looked forward to "*a new sewerage scheme*", which arrived in 1968, and more new houses.

The call for new houses had been made for many years. When Louth RDC sought the comments of Parish Councils on 'Housing of the Working Classes' in

December 1918, Withern replied that "*six new houses would be required .. many of the seven houses unoccupied were small and unsatisfactory.*" The declining population may have influenced the Parish Council when it reported to the RDC in 1925 that "*the houses are in as good a condition now as for the last years, also there are enough houses, as are required for the labour employed in the Parish, and there is also at present two empty houses in the parish.*" Louth RDC inspected 87 of the 105 houses in the parish in 1938 and recommended 31 for demolition, including Catley's Row [then known as Doctor's Row], Eight House Row and Ramscroft Cottages, all in Chalk Lane. Of the 87 inspected, 7 had WCs. Even the Chief Sanitary Inspector recommended 22 for demolition, but the outbreak of war prevented action.

In 1947 the Vyner Row houses were built by Louth RDC and in 1948 the Council again recommended 22 houses in Withern for demolition [no mud and stud houses were inspected]. By the 1960s, when the older houses were yet again scheduled for demolition, as and when they became vacant, many had been under threat for nearly 30 years. There were then five dwellings in Catley's Row [although one had been unoccupied for some years] and four in what the Lincolnshire Standard described as "*the most decrepit looking group of all*" - Ramscroft Cottages. The occupants of Eight House Row included the brothers Harold and Bert Cook, after whom the modernized terrace was named Cooks Cottages. Nearly all the houses on the 1938/48 lists were eventually restored or converted into a smaller number of modern dwellings.

Compared with only a hundred years ago, much has changed. Many fields have been merged into larger units; most of the trees which lined the roadsides have gone; the parish church has become a private house, bringing to an end 1,000 years of religious worship on the site; the mill is now a trout farm; the smaller farms, such as Corner Farm, Home Farm, The Laurels, School Farm and Willows Farm, have gone, their houses now being private residences; the Corner Farm buildings have, happily, been converted into a house; few really old houses remain; and many of the pairs of 19th century semi-detached cottages have been converted into single houses. Survivors include the Methodist Chapel, the School, the post office/stores and the Red Lion. Bungalows for the elderly [Whitethorn Way and Wells Close] and modern houses have been built along the Main Road through the village. Church Lane, leading to the church and the mill, was once lined by great trees, affording relief and shade on hot summer days; only the rectory house, the mill and the old entrance through the 'park' to Withern Hall broke the views across the fields. With modern housing development the landscape has changed.

Detail from the gravestone of John Bullivant [d1807] showing the instruments of a land surveyor.[Reproduced by permission of Mr Rex C Russell]

Detail from an 1839 gravestone, possibly that of John Horby – a late example of the 'skull and crossed bones' and the 'hourglass' - the sands of time - found on 18th century gravestones [this stone was destroyed after the sale of Withern church]. [Reproduced by permission of Mr Rex C Russell]

The Closing of the Parish Church:

While the Chapel was planning its centenary celebrations, St Margaret's was preparing for the worst; the cost of repairing the decaying fabric was beyond the resources of the parish and many essential repairs had been postponed for years. Those which had been undertaken had often been done in an inappropriate way. The condition of the church, which had been a matter of constant concern from the 1930s, led to the Diocese deciding to close it in 1973. The bell was last rung for the funeral of Lizzie Harrison in August 1976 when Laura Bullivant raced on her bicycle from the service in the Chapel to ring the parish church bell as the cortège arrived at the churchyard. The building stood empty for some years until the church and 'old' churchyard were sold for residential use.

Whether the church should have been sold is arguable, but the consequences were an affront to the families of those commemorated in the church and buried in the churchyard and a sad wrecking of an important part of Withern's history. Wall monuments to the Fitzwilliam and other families were smashed. The stained glass east window, donated by TG Tickler, was removed; part of it is now in St Peter's Church, Cleethorpes. Among the gravestones destroyed were those of:

Susanna Fitzwilliam and John Spence [1802], Benjamin Grant [1804], the Revd William Sisson [1823], Dr John Calvert [1846], Nicholas Simpson [1851], William Gresswell [1853], Naomi Chapman [1859], Edward Fenwick [1862], Edward Sisson Barker [1866], Isaac Mountain [1881], Thomas Knight [1887], William Bullivant [1888], Annie Pahud [1899] and Frank Wells [1955].

Some of the destroyed stones were examples of the Lincolnshire stonemason's craftsmanship, including those bearing winged hour-glasses and skulls and crossed bones; relatively few of this type are found today in Lindsey. One example - probably that of John Horby, who died in 1839 - was used by Rex Russell as the cover illustration for his booklet on 'Headstones in Lincolnshire' [part 1] published in 1981. While this stone has gone, some, happily, were saved and put along the access to the 'new' burial ground – and an hourglass can still be seen on the gravestone of Bell Kew Maidens, who died in 1831. The 15th century font was placed in the churchyard in a brave, but misguided, effort to preserve it.

Chapter 15:
Tothill - A Brief Look

Mediæval

The name Tothill, according to Kenneth Cameron's 'Dictionary of Lincolnshire Place-Names' [1998], has Old English roots: the personal name Tota and leah [a glade or clearing]. Although Roman coins have been found in the parish and Saxons lived here, the first information on the settlement comes from the Domesday Survey of 1086, which recorded Totele as a small but active place of about 50-100 people belonging to the Earl of Chester. The mound alongside Tothill Manor is said to be the surviving motte of a motte and bailey castle [the Earl of Chester was a builder of castles]. There was probably a watermill in 1086, when woodland would have been a significant feature of the surrounding landscape.

In the 13th century Tothill and Gayton formed one manor, belonging to Lord Willoughby de Broke, the earliest references to Gayton being in 1202 and 1206. The manor had two settlements with separate churches. Richard, the "parson of Gayton", died in 1278 and was "*buried in the church*". Michael de Suthwyk became priest at Tothill in 1323 on the "*resignation of last rector*".

In 1482 the manor had a corn mill, a fulling mill, a tile kiln and a tannery. There was also "*the grette okke of Totill*", which was quoted as a marker point in land agreements.

Names found in the manor included Barker, Crede, Dekynson, Droype, Heryng, Hormysby, Johnson, Rychardson, Skarthow and Smyth; Garbra, a family name in the manor in 1485, is found in Stain in 1601 when John Garbrore was curate of Stain church.

The Church

Built on a small hill, which provided a perfect and prominent site for a parish church, being visible over a wide area, St Mary's Church had a chequered history. The old church was in a parlous state in 1602 - "*the steple .. ys in decay and the chauncell ys in greate decay ..*", probably because the rector, Roger Smythe, was not resident in the parish for long periods.

Life was not always happy for Tothill's clergy. The restoration of the monarchy in 1660, following the collapse of the Commonwealth, saw many of the clergy suffer for their views. One of those removed from his living in 1662 was the Rector of Tothill, Thomas Gonville, who had been episcopally ordained in 1650. The Compton Census of 1676, an ecclesiastical survey, showed that, at this time, there were 36 'conformists' in Tothill, no 'papists' and no 'non-conformists'.

Following the death of the Revd Martin Bennett, Peter Desforges, a Huguenot refugee, became resident rector in 1682 and things settled down.(26) In 1707, during his incumbency, Tothill church was well kept and had a green carpet, a silk-lined cushion for the pulpit, a linen cloth for the Communion Table, two little bells, a 1638 silver cup with a lid, and a pewter flagon and patten.

The church was rebuilt in 1778, using chalk and red brick, some being taken from the old church. Erected as a simple rectangle on the stone foundations of the mediæval church, under the direction of Christopher Leek, the church had a nave, a chancel and a western turret containing one bell; there were no aisles. In 1847 Archdeacon Bonney described it as a brick chapel upon a stone foundation, with semicircular topped windows with wooden frames. The chancel was a semidecagon with a similar window at the east end, all blue slated with a cupola at the west end. The Ten Commandments and Table of Degrees of Marriage were displayed.

Despite the rebuilding and the presence of locally resident clergy, church-going was not a major part of life in Tothill. The first dissenters' meeting place in the Withern area to be registered as a place of religious worship appears to have been William North's house in Tothill, licenced in February 1791 for use by 'Methodists'. Charles Stephenson was a Methodist local preacher in 1851.

Dr Richard Yerburgh, Rector 1810-51, was non-resident, being Vicar of New and Old Sleaford. Dr Yerburgh was a kinsman of Brian Yarburgh, the 16th century occupier of Withern Hall. Among the curates he employed to run the parish was John Cordeaux, who married Elizabeth, the daughter of Richard Taylor of Tothill; their son was John Cordeaux, the ornithologist.

In 1851, when the population of Tothill was 59, its church was described as "*a small commodious Church .. but poorly attended, the average number not exceeding 6 & no resident Minister, nor any accommodation for one*". When the Revd William Grice arrived as Rector in that year, an early priority was the building of a new parsonage house to replace the old mud and stud rectory, home to the Desforges family 150 years earlier and now in "*a ruinous state*". The new Rectory, finished in 1854, housed the Rectors of Tothill for nearly a century.

The small church was again in a dilapidated state by the 1880s. In 1893-4, when William Godson was Rector, it was restored by Henry Kirk of Sleaford, who provided a new west bellcote and porch and a new east apse. Mediæval head stops were reset over the west doorway. Stained glass in the east window depicted 'The Good Shepherd'. There were three monuments: to the Revd John Stocks [d1788], Thomas Taylor [d1793] and the Revd Thomas Taylor [d1814]. The church was declared redundant in 1973 and demolished in 1980.

Tothill's gentry lived in the Manor House. In 1539 Thomas Drope was recorded as a gentleman, with servants, resident in Tothill. The parish registers, which began in 1608, record the burials of Richard Horneby Esq of South Reston and Tothill [1608], whose daughter Mary married William Ballett jr of Woodthorpe; Richard Doughty, gent [1617]; Edward Davies, gent [1632]; and Shadworth Hodgson, grandson of Martha Fitzwilliam [1788]. Martha's great-grand-daughter, Langley Grace Hodgson of Saltfleetby, was probably the last Hodgson buried in Tothill churchyard when she died in 1804.

The Manor House

The present house was built in the 17th century and refronted in the 18th, probably when the Hodgsons lived there [in 1539 a Robert Hogeson was at 'Hellowe cum Claythorp' and a John Hogeson at Calceby; Shadworth Hodgson was at Tothill in 1722]. After the Hodgsons, the Taylors were the tenants of the Manor House. In 1826

Thomas Taylor farmed two-thirds of the parish, the other farmers then being Samuel Chapman [Susanna Chapman married Nicholas Simpson II, the Withern blacksmith], Henry Reynolds, Benjamin Curtiss and Matthew Brown. In the late 1840s the tenant of the Manor House [295 acres] was William Barker, son of William Barker of Claythorpe and grandson of the Revd William Sisson; his brother Edward Barker farmed in the centre of Withern. In the 1850s John Simpson Calvert, son of the late Withern doctor, who had lived for a time with the Barkers at Claythorpe, built up a farm of 575 acres at the Manor House before moving to the Cotswolds, apparently to escape the rains he experienced in Tothill!

19th century tenants of the Manor House included the Riggall, Cocking and Rainthorpe families; in the early years of the 20th century GR Needham and Thomas Graves farmed there. Cooks Farm takes its name from the Cooks, who farmed in Tothill for many years in the 19th century. Among other farming families in the late 18th/early 19th centuries were the Barrs and the Spores.

After 700 years in his family, the Tothill estate was sold by Lord Willoughby de Broke before the Great War. The old parish of Tothill today forms part of the civil parish of Withern-with-Stain.

Tothill Manor c1908. [Reproduced by permission of Burton & Dyson, solicitors, Gainsborough/Lincolnshire Archives]

Trade

While mediæval Tothill had corn and fulling mills, employment in the 19th century was almost entirely in farm work, although, in 1849, one of the farmers, John Ridall, was also a boot and shoe maker. In 1851 William Stephenson was a "*tailor and cottager*" and John Shaw a jobbing gardener. Services were usually obtained from Authorpe, Gayton, South Reston and Withern.

There was no public house in Tothill, but there was an alehouse at Gayton Top - the Crown and Buckle - run by the Evisons in the middle of the 19th century, when it would have been popular with carters, as well as agricultural workers. It closed around 1900.

Chapter 16:
Miscellany

The following notes relate to 'facts' often quoted in Withern.

A tunnel extends from Withern Hall to the church. The late Smart Towler, who was not alone in his belief, was sure a tunnel existed and claimed to have entered it at the Hall end many years ago. When restoring the old chancel at St Margaret's House in 1997, Fred Donner made a brief excursion into the vaults, entering, via some old steps, a brick-lined passage heading in an easterly direction. The chancel of the church was probably built in the 13th/14th centuries and restored in the 15th and there were burials in these vaults for centuries. As the chancel was shortened by about 13ft in 1814, the passage would inevitably have extended beyond the present east wall of the building, which stands on foundations incorporating arches over the old tombs. The likelihood of a tunnel is neither confirmed nor disproved by what Fred saw.

There was a castle on 'Castle Hill'. No record has been found of a castle on 'Castle Hill'; indeed, little is known about this site between Louth road and Church Lane. The RCHME records, based on aerial photographs, say that "*the moat is almost square, measures 60m by 60m internally, and is defined by a substantial ditch with an inner bank.*" Mr AEB Owen comments that, if the purpose of the structure was economic, it is likely to have been built between 1066 and 1154; if it was defensive, its construction would probably have been in the 12th century when the troubles of King Stephen's reign [1135-54] affected the county.

A Fitzwilliam lady was kidnapped and ransomed. The story of a Fitzwilliam heiress being ransomed appears to be a romantic fiction to explain the family's poor financial state. There may have been confusion with other events relating to Barbary pirates who became active again after the return of Charles II [they had been severely dealt with by Admiral Blake during the Commonwealth]. In October 1668 a collection was made in Louth 'upon a brief for the poor captives of Algiers'. In 1670, when 140 men from Stepney alone were known to be captives, briefs were issued to raise ransom money. A house-to-house collection was made in Louth, £4 12s 7d being contributed by nearly 200 people; William Fitzwilliam, the Warden of Louth, gave 3s 6d.

There was a monastery at Stain. No. Stain only had a church.

Stain was destroyed by Cromwell's troops. No. Stain only had two houses in 1601. Cromwell's troops passed this way in the 1640s, yet there was a farm at Stain in 1679.

'Rogues Acre' in Stain Lane was a miscalculated 'acre'. Not so. The enclosure award of 1838-40 gave the Parish Clerk this half-acre of land, which was probably in the area of his previous allotment. It had not always been such a long way from the village, for, in 1829 the Clerk, who lived in the village, wrote a note lamenting that, when he became Clerk, "*the clerk then ad one aker of good land. I made it, but they took it from me and gave me a litel bater than 2 roud of very poor land which was no hend of expens to me to get aney thing of it and hade it almost one mile forther from home .. and if it was not for the kindness of the minnister I would not be clark hear at all.*"

There was a pub where Red Lion Cottages stand. Ted Jackson and Wally White recall an iron grille in a passage in the old building [which stood alongside Main Road until c1960], the sort of grille which might have been a serving hatch for those who did not wish to enter the alehouse premises.

The Justices appear to have licensed two alehouses in Withern between 1792 and 1828 - the Red Lion and The Three Tuns, of which Francis Barker and John Pocklington were the respective publicans in 1828. Barker had married the widow of John Spence, the Red Lion publican, in 1805 and was publican and brewer at The Red Lion 1805-c1831.

Thomas Marshall appears to have succeeded James Porter at the White House, a small Withern farm next to the Red Lion, following Porter's death in 1827.

In 1835 Pigot's Directory listed Barker as a *"brewer"* and Thomas Marshall as licensee of The Red Lion. The consistency of the Spence/Barker Land Tax Assessment and Church Rents between 1780 and 1832 suggests that the old Red Lion Cottages building probably housed the Red Lion Inn, because Francis Barker [licensee of the Red Lion in 1828] was only a brewer in 1832, while Thomas Marshall [a butcher with a low level of Church Rents in 1828] had a Tax Assessment and Church Rents higher than Barker in 1832. Legislation passed in the 1830's reversed the licensing policy developed in the preceding centuries, the Beer Act of 1830 removing many controls introduced under previous acts. As it became possible for any householder assessed to the poor rate to sell beer, ale and cider without a licence from local justices by taking out an excise licence granted by the Excise authorities, it is possible Barker, a brewer, continued to sell beer during the 1830s.

At the time of the Tithe Award [1838] "Francis Barker, brewer", was living in the old Red Lion Cottages building, but he and the house do not appear by then to have been involved in the brewing trade. Barker, who fathered an illegitimate son in 1832 [he has descendants in New Zealand], had died by 1841. The house was then converted into cottages.

Text Notes

1 A league was about three miles; woodland probably extended from the 'Alford way' to the Beesby-Claythorpe road and the river to Woodthorpe.
2 Richard de Welle and his wife Elizabeth were buried in the priory of the Carmelite Friars at Doncaster.
3 Margaret Beauchamp was the widow of John Beaufort, 1st Duke of Somerset (d1444), and a descendant of John of Gaunt.
4 Reminders of the mediæval church are: a fragment of 13th century tracery; early 15th century octagonal columns; part of the 15th century chancel south wall; a 3-light window; and the font [15th century, says Pevsner], now in the churchyard.
5 See *Monumental Incised Slabs in Lincolnshire*, FA Greenhill, 1986; stone now at Louth Museum.
6 In the hall [the main living room] of Stain manor house were a long table, a little table, a form, four chairs, a press [cupboard], a dishboard [dresser] and a bench board: for cooking over the fire there were a gallibawke, hooks, tongs, etc, as well as brass pots, a postenet, pans, cauldrons and a wooden trough containing old irons [the gallibawke indicates that the fire was in a fireplace - probably brick - with a chimney and no longer in a central hearth in the hall].

  In Skipwith's parlour was a framed table – i.e. a joined table, with the board fixed to a supporting frame, a type which had only come into use around 1540. There were carpets on the tables, buffet stools, mock velvet cushions, a pair of playing tables, silver spoons and a painted cloth - all reflecting the home of a wealthy man.

The bed parlour contained, inter alia, a truss-bed [a solid bedstead], a trandle bed, two feather beds, coverings, a press, 2 shifts, bed and table linen, and 2 maidens' beds.

7   Brian Yarburgh, son of Charles Yarburgh and his 2nd wife Elizabeth Newcomen. Charles' 1st wife, Agnes Skipwith, was aunt to Mary Skipwith, wife of George Fitzwilliam [d 1560].

8   In 1593 Arthur Hall MP for Grantham, sold the manor of Woodthorpe, acquired by Hall from the Cavendishes, to John Ballett. The Ballett family owned Woodthorpe for about 300 years. Charles Ballett [bapt Withern 1635, son of Charles Ballett of Alford and Sarah, daughter of Thomas Newcomen of Withern] was 'late of Clements Inn, Middlesex' when he died in 1703. A century later a Miss Ballett married a Mr Brereton; their daughter had, by a Mr Fletcher, an illegitimate son, John Ballett Fletcher of Woodthorpe, Lincs, and Pagham, Sussex. JB Fletcher married Sarah Vere, youngest daughter of John Holland Esq of Skendleby Thorpe in 1844. In 1889 'William Holland Ballot Fletcher' held land in Woodthorpe.

9   Robert Vyner's wife Eleanor was, by her 1st marriage, the mother of Charles Anderson, 1st Baron Yarborough.

10 Lady Mary was daughter of Earl de Grey KG and niece of the 1st Earl of Ripon, Prime Minister in 1827. The forebears of the two Earls, the sons of the 2nd Lord Grantham, included the last non-Royal Duke of Kent.

11 In gratitude for the safe return of five sons from the Great War, and as a tribute to his ancestors' lives in Withern, TG Tickler placed an east window in the chancel of the Church. After the sale of the church, the window was removed; part of it is now in St Peter's Church, Cleethorpes.

12 Samuel Desforges was a descendant of the Revd Peter Desforges, the 17th century rector of Tothill.

13 Strubby parish had a similar problem; when its church was rebuilt in 1857 the whole of the old church, apart from the south arcade, fell when the roof was removed.

14 William Sisson was curate for Dr Vyner at Authorpe from 1787; he resided in Withern Rectory for 30 years.

15 William Phillips Vyner [1806-78] was grandson of the Revd Thos Vyner, non-resident Rector of Authorpe 1760-66, and nephew of Dr Thos Vyner [1753-1804], a prebend or canon of Canterbury Cathedral and also non-resident Rector of Authorpe. His father was Robert Vyner [1765-1823], barrister-at-law of Lincoln's Inn and legal adviser to the Gautby family, who had married Laura, daughter and heiress of the late Phillips Glover of Wispington, in 1799; they had 12 children. William, the 2nd surviving son, became Rector of Withern and Authorpe. His widowed mother took her younger children to Germany for their education: Delicia Ann married General Count von Blumenthal; Edmund became Aide-de-Camp to Duke Ernst II of Saxe-Coburg-Gotha, the brother of the Prince Consort; Henry was a Prussian Guards officer, then Paymaster in the Turkish Contingent in the Crimean War, and later Asst Military Auditor on General Sir Thos Ashburnham's staff in China [Henry was staying at Withern Rectory at the time of the 1851 Census]; Arthur and Frederick, naval officers, settled at Tumut, New South Wales, Australia [Vyner's Creek, at Yarrara Station, is named after Frederick]. Margaret Anne Vyner, Arthur's wife, wrote to the poet Tennyson from Tumut in 1855 explaining how his poetry comforted her in the isolation of the Australian bush.

16 The 'National Society for Promoting th0e Education of the Poor in the Principles of the Church of England', founded 1811. The School House was demolished c1986.

17 The father of William Gresswell sr was a grazier in Lusby. His mother, Elizabeth, was sister of John Elsey who farmed Aby Grange [1780] before moving to Low Toynton.

18 John Chapman, son of John and Naomi, married Jane Ailsby of Strubby in Hull in 1877. After their wedding they had what Jane described in her diary as "*a nice party*" in Strubby with "*Mr and Mrs Chapman, Mrs Farrow and Mrs Coupland, my Father and Mother and the rest of the family*" (information from Andy Chapman, Australia].

19 When Thomas Marwood died in 1856 his gravestone bore the epitaph: "*One morning I missed him on the accustomed round, Along the path and near his favourite tree another came. Nor yet behind the mound nor up the path nor up the road was he.*"

20 'Rantanning', 'riding the stang' or 'riding the skimmington' an ancient custom by which popular disapproval was expressed towards people who had offended by anti-social or immoral behaviour [see: 'The Mayor of Casterbridge' by Thomas Hardy]. The last recorded Rantanning in Lincolnshire was carried out in Scamblesby in 1930.

21 Dr WC Calthrop, born Gosberton, educated Boston Grammar School, a Captain in the 10th Light Infantry, practised in Crowland and Spilsby before coming to Withern. His son, Col Carr-Calthrop, born in Withern, was a surgeon in the Indian Medical Service.

22 A Fred Mountain photograph in the *Lincolnshire Standard*, June 1984.

23 Withern Cricket Club folded in 1961; its assets were handed to the 1st Withern Scout Troop.

24 The last two machines owned by the Harrison family were made by Wallis and Steevens at Basingstoke, one in 1880 [No T158], and the other in 1901. The latter, acquired in 1903, was, with its older partner, the mainstay of their operations until Harrisons went out of business in July 1929. At the closing down sale the T158 was sold to J Drakes of Stainton-le-Vale and the 1901 machine [No 2538] to G Simons of Maltby-le-Marsh, being licensed by Simons until 1943.

25 The 'Withern Surgery' operated here until the Alford practice closed it in 2003. A doctor's surgery existed in Withern for about 180 years. Dr Lord died in Berkshire in 2003.

26 Peter Desforges was born in France c 1654 and arrived in London as a Protestant refugee in 1681 [he is said to have arrived at the Tower Wharf in London in September 1681 disguised as a woman]. A protégé of Lord Alington, Constable of the Tower of London, who had spent several years in exile at Blois in the Loire Valley during the early part of Cromwell's Commonwealth, Desforges may also have known the Verney family in exile, among whom were the lords Willoughby de Broke, lords of the manor of Tothill. Ordained deacon Dec 1681 and priest June 1682 by the Bishop of London, he was licensed to Tothill by the Bishop of Lincoln, on 19 January 1682. He was also instituted Rector of South Reston on 29 Sept 1688 by the Bishop of Lincoln. He married twice and had a large family. When he died in 1725 he was buried at Tothill.

Mr Ted Milson

APPENDIX I
Brief Notes on some of Withern's Houses Past and Present

BROOK FARM
Farm 1686 [tenant R Keale]. House/older buildings pre-1840. A Vyner farm: tenants the Wells family c1809-c1919.

CARROTTS CORNER
House & neighbour built c1870 by William Carrott. Once known as Field or Bleak House.

COLCROFT HOUSE
Was two houses, built c1862 by Isaac Mountain in Colcroft field.

COOKS COTTAGES
Originally 8 cottages, built 1840s. Wilson's Row [1851-81]/Marshall's Row [1891]/Eight House Row [1960s].

DAROS
Storey butcher's shop stood at the roadside here in 1840; later became cottages [demolished]. Rebuilt for Miss Enderby in 20th century.

FAIRVIEW
Stovin farm [demolished]; Wm Harrison and John Tyson 19th cent. tenants.

GLEBE HOUSE, THE [Old Rectory]
A rectory house existed 1454. 17th century house "*built with wood .. walls mud and clay,*" roof "*covered with straw*" was "*fac'd almost all round with brick*" in 1746. Late 18th century renovation removed the mud walls; sash windows added 1820. Partly rebuilt, with new outbuildings, 1836-40 and extended 1911.

GRANGE FARM
Heart of the 17th century Stovin estate, farmed by Thomas Mountain c1790-1816/Coulams 1816-1880/Elmitt Payne to 1919. In 1817 an "*excellent farm,*" the house "*convertible into a pleasant Marine Residence for a Gentleman's Family.*"

GRANGE FARM COTTAGE
Formerly two cottages. Wall plate [RSM 1855] marks it as the survivor of three sets of Stain Lane cottages built by Richard Stovin Maw.

HAVEN, THE
Site of first Methodist Chapel [1809] and adjacent cottage ["*baker's shop and oven*" 1836]; the chapel became a warehouse 1875.

HILLCREST
Successor to old Vyner farmhouse. Risdale farm 1851, later occupied by Amos Bullivant. Rebuilt c1938.

HOLLYDENE
Thomas Askey's shop 1838; Harrison home 1876-1930.

HOME FARM
Successor to a thatched house [demolished 1938]. Kirman farm 1832; Bullivant home since 1860s.

HOMELEIGH
Once a thatched house; Richard Young was butcher here 1841.

LAURELS, THE
Older part of the house is the surviving building of a Fitzwilliam/Stovin farm [100 acres in 1817]. Farmed by Loughtons [19th century]/Richard Marshall 1913-18/Mountains 1918-77.

LONGLANDS
House and yard 1680. "*Good brick built farm house*" 1804. New buildings for JC Drewery [wall plates RSM 1853/JCD 1854]. In 1920 had sledge roof on rear of house, brick crew yard and stables.

LUPIN COTTAGE/RETFORD HOUSE/JASMINE/MEERSBROOK
Built c1875 by William Askey.

MANOR, THE
Built c1670. Fitzwilliam home in 17th/18th centuries. Irregular 5-bay front and 2-storey gabled porch; altered on several occasions. Farmed by Grants 1815-40s/George Kelk 1856-c78/Arthur Enderby c1888-1940/Elmitt Rutter.

OLD FORGE, THE
The outbuildings bear testimony to the smithy [old house demolished].

ORCHARD FARM [formerly Twigmore House]
Farm in 17th century; bought by George Stovin 1709. Fenwick house 1838. John Larder grocer/farmer 1851. Home of William Clark and family 1900s.

PARK FARM
Probably created in 17th century. Vyner farm, known as 'Fishpond House'. Farmed by Thomas Showler 1790s/J Desforges 1798-1820/Robinsons 1820-68/JR Desforges 1868-75/WW Wells 1875-1920/Burkitts 1920+.

PUMP COTTAGE [Catley's Row]
Row of cottages built in 1830s by Joseph Catley.

RAMSCROFT
Once 4 cottages, two [Wells Cottages] built in 1860, two in 1870s. Known as Ramscroft 1881.

RED LION
See Miscellany section; inn rebuilt in 1860s.

RED LION COTTAGES
Site of a house, the home of Francis Barker 1838; cottages 1840 [demolished]. Replaced by modern houses.

ROSE COTTAGE
Built by Thomas White c1862; originally two houses.

SCHOOL FARM [Woodthorpe]
A small farm, its lands associated with Queen Elizabeth's Grammar School, Alford [demolished].

SINDY
Once a thatched Vyner farmhouse. Farmed by Benjamin Grant 1780 and James Enderby jr 1830s. Made into two cottages c1870; later one house.

STAIN HILL FARM
Brick house, once thatched, had tin roof by mid-20th century. Brick outbuildings; barns tarred wood [demolished].

SUNNYHOLME
Three Tuns Inn 1792. In 1838 had Askey's shop [Hollydene] on one side, Poor Houses on the other, and Vear's farm behind. After the inn closed c1876 it became a carpenter's shop and later a bakery.

THREE ACRES [formerly Virginia Cottage]
John Stephenson's home 1838. Earlier name derived from house being covered in Virginia creeper.

VILLAGE SHOPS
Post Office: building here 1838, possibly house of Edward Orry or his father Maddison Orry, owner of the Village Stores. Cockett shop in 1860s, Askey shop in 1870s. JS Thorn's 'Withern Supply Stores' [Post Office 1906+].

Village Stores: warehouse area to rear of shop was originally a single storey partly mud & stud structure, probably 18th century; considerably rebuilt. Orry's Village Stores [Maddison Orry was in Withern 1809 and name Orry is carved roughly in one of the joists]. Probably the shop of John Wright in 1790s, and possibly of Thomas Dales before that. Congregation of Primitive Methodists may have met in a room here in 1840s. Post office 1870-1906. Willson's 'Village Stores & Post Office' 1896-1906.

WESTFIELD HOUSE
Built in the 1860s, probably as two cottages.

WHARFEDALE COTTAGE
House between shops, formerly three cottages built in 1850s.

THE WHITE HOUSE

Thos Marshall had a small farm in 1838 for which this appears to have been the farmhouse. Later a cottage attached to Red Lion Farm.

WILLOWS

Vyner farm. Home of the Atkin family 1840-1915, then the Searby family.

WILSON'S/GOLLINGS' COTTAGE

During demolition [1980] cottage in front of Karatangi was found to be thatched mud & stud, bricked over and its roof pantiled in 19th century. It was probably Withern's last timber-framed mud & stud house when built c1790. Occupiers included the Cotton, Wilson and Gollings families. Reconstructed as 'Withern Cottage' at Church Farm Museum, Skegness.

WITHERN CORNER [FARM]

Fitzwilliam farm 1686. Bought by George Stovin 1709. Later owners John Desforges, Revd Dr J Parkinson and Payne family.

WITHERN HALL

This was the oldest house in Withern, built c1550, brick with walls 3ft thick, low oak-beamed ceilings and some Tudor windows. Fitzwilliam home in late 16th/early 17th centuries. "Mannor house" called 'The Hall' 1664. Main farm in Vyner Estate. Enlarged in 1880s, it had 3 staircases leading to 10 bedrooms [demolished].

WOODLANDS

Probably built by Dr William Calthrop c1847-50; no house on this site on 1838-40 Tithe Award and Enclosure maps.

APPENDIX II
Farms 1838 and 1851

In the 19th century farms changed in size as lands were reallocated by the landowners [the farm owners in 1838 = V Robert Vyner; S R Stovin Maw; A Alford Grammar School; F Edward Fenwick; P Revd Dr J Parkinson].

The farms were, in roughly descending order of size:

Farms [100acres+]		1838			1851	
		Acres	Tenant		Acres	Tenant
V	Hall Fm	361	Richard Grant		606	William Grant
S	Grange Fm	511	Joseph Coulam		321	George Coulam
V	Park Farm	186	Samuel Robinson		230	Thomas Robinson
V	'Village fm'	151	James Enderby sr		220	Edward Barker
S	The Manor	112	William Grant		197	Joseph Coulam
V	Brook Fm	154	John Wells		160	John Wells
S	Longlands		[with Grange Fm]		135	JC Drewery

Medium sized farms [50-99 acres]:

V	Sindy	89	James Enderby jr		98	James Enderby
P	Corner Fm	85	George T Grant			
S	Laurels	40	James Loughton		83	James Loughton
A	School Fm	36	Robert Lucas		60	George Hutchings

Smaller farms [20-49 acres]:

V	Vear's fm	29	George Vear		49	George Vear
V	Red Lion	32	Thomas Marshall		46	Thomas Marshall
V	Willows	23	John Desforges jr		45	Richard Atkin
V	Home Fm	18	John Kirman		31	John Kirman
S	Fairview	14	William Harrison		20	John Tyson

Cottage farms [under 20 acres] included:

		Acres		Acres	
V	Chalk Lane fm	16	Thomas Davy		
F	Orchard Fm			15	John Larder
S	Gold Lane fm	10	Richard Young	14	William Jarvis
V	Brookfield	14	John Bromfield		J Brumfield
V	Hillcrest		John Desforges jr	13	John Risdal
V	The Forge	13	Nicholas Simpson		Nicholas Simpson
V	Stain Hill		William Maidens	9	Elizabeth Maidens

Some of the 1838 farms have disappeared from the map; six still function. Barfen, a post-enclosure farm, did not exist in 1838.

1881, 1913 and 1926

Later occupants of Withern's farms included:

Larger farms [over 100 acres]:

	Acres	Tenant 1881	Farmer 1913	Farmer 1926
Withern Hall	830	Walliss T Wells	William Rutter	Aner Scargall
Barfen Farm		[with Withern Hall until 1920]		Fred Scargall
The Manor	350	Mrs E Badley	Arthur Enderby	Arthur Enderby
Longlands Cott		[with The Manor until 1918, then with Longlands]		
Grange Farm	240	[bailiff]	Elmitt Payne	Jas Pocklington
Park Farm	230	Wm W Wells	Wm W Wells	Charles Burkitt
Red Lion Fm	230	Mrs MA Marshall	JT Marshall	Charles Berry
Brook Farm	175	John Wells	execs J Wells	E Millson
Longlands	171	Mrs C Drewery	Elijah Scargall	Alf Mountain
Laurels	127	Wm Loughton	R Marshall	Fred Mountain

Medium sized farms [50-99 acres]:

	Acres	Tenant 1881	Farmer 1913	Farmer 1926
Corner Fm	66	R Gibbons	Thomas Payne	Thomas Payne
School Farm	57	Thos Hutchings		

Smaller farms [20-49 acres]:

	Acres	Tenant 1881	Farmer 1913	Farmer 1926
Willows	38	Richard Atkin	Richard Atkin	AE Searby
Karatangi	26	Wm Wilson	Jas W Wilson	Jas W Wilson

Cottage farms [10-20 acres] included:

	Acres	Tenant 1881	Farmer 1913	Farmer 1926
Carrott's Corn.	13	William Carrott	Wm Carrott	Wm Carrott jr
The Forge	12	Barth. White	AE Searby	Chas Chatterton
Hillcrest	11	William Risdale	Amos Bullivant	
Home Farm	12	Wm Bullivant	Wm Bullivant	Wm Bullivant
Ivy Cott/Failte	9	William Jarvis	Joseph Norton	Joseph Norton
Stain Hill		Christ. Maidens	Chas H Massey	CW Thorndike

Today only four farms have resident farmers. The smaller farms have passed into history and the Manor farm has been absorbed by Red Lion Farm.

Appendix III
Rectors of Withern 1500-1920

1500-1507	Thomas Madiowe, presented by Cecily, Viscountess de Welle.
1508-1509	Stephen Hawys, presented by The Crown.
1510-1542	Simon Weldon LLB, presented by The Crown.
1542-1551	George Billesby, presented by Arthur Dymoke by grant of the heirs of the lords of Welle.
1552-1579	John Taylor, presented by The Crown. Resided West Barkwith; "ignorant of Latin" and "little versed in sacred learning."
1579-1580	Robert Sarrot, presented by William Fitzwilliam. Res: Withern.
1580-1581	William Wickham DD [Bishop of Lincoln 1584-95], presented by Herbert Pelham.
1582-1608	Nicholas Madison, presented by William Fitzwilliam. Also Rector of Trusthorpe. Buried Withern [in chancel].
1608-1632	Philip Pregion MA, presented by John Pregion by grant of William Fitzwilliam. Resided Withern.
1632-1644	John Walker MA, presented by George Walker by grant of Sir George Fitzwilliam.
1644-1671	Robert Morton MA, presented by William Fitzwilliam. Master, Alford Grammar School. Buried Withern.
1671-1688	Thomas Cooper MA, presented by Thomas Newcomen & George Fitzwilliam. Resided and buried Withern.
1688-1691	Simon Smyth(es) MA, presented by Thomas Newcomen. Said to be buried at Withern.
1691-1693	Samuel Adcock MA, presented by George Fitzwilliam. Rector of Gayton-le-Marsh 1670-93. Buried Gayton.
1694-1700	Robert White MA, presented by George Fitzwilliam. Buried Withern.
1701-1725	William Jones BA, presented by George Fitzwilliam. Resided Withern Rectory. Buried Withern.
1726-1771	John Marriott BA, presented by Robert Vyner. Vicar of Theddlethorpe All Saints 1729-68. Resided Withern Rectory. Left Withern 1771. Died in Finchingfield, Essex. Curate: 1764-72 Basil R Burkit [Withcall]
1772-1789	Simon Adams LLB, presented by Robert Vyner. Non-resident. Curates: 1774-1782 John Hayward Smith [S Ormsby] 1785-1794 Thomas Taylor [Tothill]
1789-1836	John Mounsey BA, JP, presented by Robert Vyner. Rector of Gautby 1783-1836 & Authorpe 1806-36. JP for Lincs. Resided Gautby. Died 1836. Officiating Minister 1794-1821: William Sisson, Vicar of Goulceby 1799 & Burwell 1811. Curate: Belleau 1782-1806 & Authorpe 1787-1821. Resided Authorpe Rectory 1790 and Withern Rectory c1794-1823. Buried Withern. Officiating Minister 1821-36: William Lowther Sisson (Sisson-Wayet) BA, born Authorpe. Resided Withern Rectory and later Horncastle. Buried Withern.

1836-1877	William Phillips Vyner BA, JP, presented by Robert Vyner. Rector of Authorpe 1836-77. Rural Dean of Calcewath. Resided Withern Rectory. Died 1878. Buried Louth.
1877-1907	Frederick A Glover MA, LLB, MusB, JP, presented by HFC Vyner. Rural Dean, Calcewath No 1. Resided Withern Rectory. Died c1909 in Bristol.1907-1919 C Noel Swayne MA, presented by RCdeG Vyner. Brother of Bishop Swayne. Resided Withern Rectory. Died 1948.
1919-1922	Samuel Frost, presented by Lady Mary Compton-Vyner.

Rectors of Stain 1500-1687

1500	John Gooderick, presented by Sir John Skipwith, as ward of Thomas Fitzwilliam.
1523-32	Richard White. Died 1532.
1532	John Richardson
1541-51	Thomas Gaytley. Resigned 1551.
1551	Richard Candelsby.
1555	John Thorpe.
	[The Rectory of Stain may have been vacant 1559-85]
1585	Samuel Willingham BA, Vicar of Water Eaton, Yaxley, Hunts. Curate: John Garbrore 1601.
1631-33	Thomas Codde, clerk, MA, presented by Henry Bradley, by reason of a grant from William Fitzwilliam.
1633	Henry Neave, clerk. Patron: the bishop by lapse.
1661-87	Charles Asfordby, who was Rector of Mablethorpe St Mary 1661-87. He was the last Rector of Stain.

Rectors of Tothill 1600-1920

c1600	Roger Smythe
1627	Thomas Powell, presented by Lord Broke.
pre 1645	George Carr BA.
1656	John Passmore BA, presented by Dame Katherine Verney, guardian of Grenville Verney.
1658	Thomas Gonville MA, presented by Sir Thomas Denman.
1662	Martin Bennett, presented by the Verney guardians.
1682	Peter Desforges, presented by Lord Alington. Died 1725. Resided in the old Tothill Rectory.
1725	William Bowes.
pre 1758	John Stocks. Died 1788. Buried Tothill. Curate 1786-1814: Thomas Taylor.
1788	John Lloyd, inducted 8 November 1788. Non-resident.
1810	Richard Yerburgh DD, MA, presented by Lord Willoughby de Broke; Vicar of New & Old Sleaford. Non-resident. Curate c1830-45: John Cordeaux.
1851	William Grice BA, presented by Lord Willoughby de Broke. Built and resided in the new Tothill Rectory.
1890	William Godson. Res: Tothill Rectory. Died 1910. Bur: Tothill.
1910	John James Thomson MA, BD. [see Authorpe]. Res: Tothill Rectory. Died 1921. Buried Tothill.

Rectors of Authorpe 1720-1920

1719	Richard White. Died 1758.
1760	Thos Vyner MA, presented by Robt Vyner. Non-res. Died 1766.
c1780	Dr Thomas Vyner LLD, presented by Robert Vyner. Admitted to prebend or canonry of Canterbury Cathedral 1782. Vicar of East Peckham, Kent, 1789. Non-res. Died 1804.
1804	Thomas Morse.
1806	John Mounsey [see Withern].
1836	William Phillips Vyner [see Withern].
1877	James Foster BA, BCL Durham.
1890	Alfred H Wimberley.
1902	Reginald Hewes Allot Quinet ["The Glebe House, now occupied by the Rector, was entirely restored by RC de G Vyner esq in 1901" - Kelly's Directory 1905].
1908	John James Thomson MA, BD [see Tothill].

Appendix IV
Some Surnames found in Withern before the 19th Century

14th century:
Burdon, Chubbe, Cockewold, Grumpthorp, Herholm, Howys, Mannyng and Miley.

16th century:
Blanchard, Buston, Chapman, Cram, Cramer, Downer, East, Fitzwilliam, Foster, Fox, Freeman, Goodwin, Green, Greenall, Madison, Mawer, Melton, Myllisent, Priestwell, Raithby, Richardson, Robinson, Smith, Stones, Thorndike, Thornton, Underwell and Yerburgh.

17th century:
Avison, Barker, Barkwith, Blakey, Bland, Bullivant, Burton, Carden, Chauntrie, Cook, Copland, Cotton, Dickenson, Emerson, Etherington, Everin, Gauntlet, Hall, Harrison, Hodgson, Keale, Kelk, Key, Kidd, Lamyman, Leach, Leary, Marshall, Palfreyman, Palmer, Preston, Rosengrave, Saunderson, Simpson, Sleight, Spendley, Stampe, Starbrough, Stocks, Stovin, Stow, Talkes, Warmouth, White and Wright.

18th century:
Adlard, Andrews, Archer, Badeley, Bontoft, Borman, Clark, Dales, Desforges, Dinsdale, Dowse, Emmitt, Enderby, Finch, Grant, Gresswell, Griffin, Gunnil, Holland, Johnson, Julian, Kirman, Lancaster, Lucas, Manby, Mountain, Porter, Showler, Spence, Storey, Swinn, Tickler, Upton, Vear, Walmsley, Wells, West and Willows.

Less common surnames found in Withern and Tothill have included Acrill, Basker, Heryng, Pinsent, Purle and Tantalot.

Appendix V
Roll of Honour and War Memorial

Those who died in the Great War 1914-18:

Richard Branston   1916   L/Sergeant, 10th ['Chums'] Battn, Lincs Regt, aged 34. Brewery Orchard Cem, Nord, France.

William Brumpton   1916   L/Corporal, 1st Battn, Lincs Regt, aged 20. Gordon Dump Cem, Somme, France [Flaxmill Cottages].

George Cross   1918   Private, 2nd/6th Battn, N Staffs Regt, aged 20. Arras Memorial, Pas de Calais, France [Tothill].

Arthur Enderby   1917   Private, 54th Battn, Canadian Inf. (C Ont. Regt), aged 34; served S African War. Menin Gate Memorial, Ieper, Belgium [b Withern Manor].

Charles Lane

Herbert Lane   1917   Private, 8th Battn, Lincs Regt. Hooge Crater Cemetery, Ieper, Belgium.

Robt Arthur Massey   1916   Joined Army 1 March. Died of pneumonia 16 June, aged 27; buried Withern with Scottish Horse firing party [formerly of Stain].

Fred Searby   1916   L/Corporal, 1st Battn, Lincs Regt, aged 25. Fricourt British Cemetery, Somme, France [of S Reston; b Withern].

J William Searby   1916   Sapper, 202nd Field Co, RE, aged 28. Caterpillar Valley Cemetery, Longueval, Somme, France [son of Fred Searby, Withern].

William Stones

William Ward MM   1918   Private, 20th Battn, Durham LI. Zantvoorde Brit. Cemetery, Zonnebeke, Belgium [Military Medal].

Ronald Webster   1917   Driver, 128th Field Co, RE, aged 27. Railway Dugouts Burial Ground, Ieper, Belgium.

Maurice White   1918   Private, 1st Battn, Lincs Regt, aged 30. Abbeville Commun Cemetery Extn, Somme, France [son of John William White, Withern].

Willie White   Private, Yorks & Lancs Regt [b Jul 1887 Strubby: brother of Maurice White]

Wounded [recorded in the School Log Book]:

Albert Edwd Gosling   1917   Driver, S Staffs Regt.

Ernest Lane   1918   Private, 7th Battn, Lincs Regt.

P Marwood   1917   Gunner, Royal Field Artillery.

HV Slayton   1918   Lieut, Middlesex Regt, invalided from Service.

J Urry   1918   Private, gassed.

C Ward   1917   L/Corporal, West Yorkshire Regt.

Walliss Thos Wells   1915   Australian Light Horse, wounded [Dardenelles].

Honours [recorded in the School Log Book]:

E Watson MM   1918   Private, 1st Battn, Norfolk Regt. Military Medal.

Sister Lilian Webster   QANS. Royal Red Cross 2nd Class [ARRC].

Those who died in the Second World War 1939-45:

Fred Searby   1944   Corporal, 6th Battn, Lincs Regt. Cassino War Cemetery, Italy.

Charles E Westerby   1944   Rifleman, 9th Battn, Cameronians [Scottish Rifles], aged 19. Leopoldsburg War Cemetery, Limburg, Belgium.

Appendix VI
Withern School Pupils 1871

The following list of pupils is taken from the Inspector's Report, 31 January 1871, quoted in the school logbook:

No.	Name	Age	Year	Month	Attendance	Class
1	Sarah Borman	7	66	6	321	6
2	Sarah Skelton	7	68	3	417	6
3	Mary Tyson	7	70	5	255	6
4	Elizabeth Searby	8	68	2	250	6
5	Fanny Horn	7	70	4	258	6
6	Harriet Adlard	8	70	5	233	6
7	Walliss Wells	7	66	4	296	6
8	Joseph Keal	9	70	5	288	6
9	Frederick Keal	8	70	5	272	6
10	Anne Fussy	10	69	10	350	5
11	Susan. Mountain	8	67	4	437	5
12	Ellen Brown	8	68	6	427	5
13	Mary Buttler	8	68	9	423	5
14	Eliza Green	8	66	7	368	5
15	Charlotte Risdal	8	68	3	382	5
16	Fanny Tompkins	10	70	5	233	5
17	George White	8	67	1	430	5
18	Amos Bullivant	8	67	3	367	5
19	George Towning	10	70	2	214	5
20	Joseph Topliss	9	66	5	294	5
21	John Fussy	9	70	2	378	5
22	William Birkett	9	69	8	320	5
23	Jane Horn	11	69	6	235	5
24	Mary Mountain	9	67	5	431	4
25	Mary Borman	9	65	4	257	4
26	Charlotte Dowse	13	69	1	319	4
27	Charles Knight	9	66	4	436	4
28	John Clarke	9	65	4	377	4
29	Charles Buttler	9	68	5	404	4
30	Wright Allett	12	63	6	251	4
31	George Allett	10	64	7	370	4
32	Anderson Dowse	10	55	4	408	4
33	John Adlard	10	70	5	213	4
34	Annie Carrott	10	69	6	351	3
35	Mary Skelton	11	66	4	390	3
36	Sarah Oliver	10	67	3	405	3
37	Louisa Willson	11	66	12	359	3
38	Martha Borman	11	63	6	352	3
39	Lucy Topliss	12	64	2	277	3
40	Jane Simpson	13	69	10	356	3
41	Anne Skelton	13	69	10	305	3
42	John Evison	11	66	5	335	3
43	Joseph Broddle	11	66	5	338	3
44	Henry Kennington	11	65	4	417	3
45	Henry Simons	10	67	5	290	3
46	Thomas Bond	11	69	10	344	3

47	Elias Hutton	12	70	1	259	3
48	William Hodgson	13	69	10	219	3
49	George Jackson	12	70	1	230	3
50	Thomas Parker	12	70	1	230	3
51	Sarah Simons	11	64	4	383	2
52	Ruth Douse	12	65	4	217	2
53	Charles Carrott	12	68	6	336	2
54	Charles Mountain	11	64	6	373	2
55	Allen Millson	12	67	4	376	2
56	RV Calthrop	11	68	1	364	2
57	Edward Prigeon	13	68	10	206	1
U6	Martha Brown	6	68	6	421	
	Mary Risdal	6	69	5	324	
	Rose Marwood	6	70	4	297	
	Alice Tyson	6	70	5	223	
	John Borman	5	68	10	427	
	Charles Coupland	6	69	5	364	
	George Green	5	70	2	363	
	Solomon Mountain	5	69	3	345	
	Thomas Whattam	6	70	4	245	
	Charles Adlard	5	70	5	229	
	Thomas Brown	4	70	5	296	

Appendix VII
The Chief Lords of Withern

The owners of the main manor in Withern with approximate dates:

Date	Name	Notes
1086-1114	Rademer	son of Gilbert.
1114-	Walter de Welle	son of Rademer.
?	William de Welle	son of WdeW; buried Bardney.
		[m. dau of Walter de Gand]
-1206	Robert de Welle	son of WdeW (1).
1206-1241	William de Welle (2)	son of RdeW (1); bur. Greenfield.
1241-1260	Robert de Welle (2)	son of WdeW (2).
1260-1289	William de Welle (3)	son of RdeW (2); bur. Greenfield.
1289-1311	Adam, Baron de Welle	son of RdeW (2); bur. Greenfield.
1311-1320	Robert, 2nd B de Welle	son of 1st Baron.
1320-1344	Adam, 3rd B de Welle	son of 1st Baron; bur. Greenfield.
1344-1361	John, 4th B de Welle	son of 3rd Baron.
1361-1421	John, 5th B de Welle	son of 4th Baron.
1421-1461	Lionel, 6th B de Welle	gdson of 5th B; killed at Towton.
	[title and property forfeited to the Crown 1461]	
1467-1470	Richard, 7th B de Welle	son of 6th B; executed 1470
	[estates restored to him 1467; but again forfeited	
	to the Crown after his execution]	
	[m. dau of 6th Ld Willoughby d'Eresby].	
1482-1485	Sir Richard Hastings, 8th B de Welle 1482 in right of wife Joan,	
	dau of 7th B de Welle.	
1485-1499	John, 9th B de Welle;	son of 6th B; cr. Viscount 1486;
	cr. Viscount de Welle	KG 1488; title/estatesestates restored by
		Henry VII; bur. Westminster Abbey
	[m. Cecily, dau of Edward IV].	
1499-1510	The Crown	
1510-1579	Heirs of the de Welles	
1579-1597	William Fitzwilliam	of Mablethorpe; buried Withern.
1597-1637	Sir Geo. Fitzwilliam	son of WF; knight 1606; buried Withern.
1637-1678	William Fitzwilliam (2)	son of Sir GF; Warden of Louth; buried Louth.
1678-1682	George Fitzwilliam (2)	son of WF (2); buried Withern.
1682-1704	George Fitzwilliam (3)	son of GF (2); buried Withern.
1704-1724	William Fitzwilliam (3)	son of GF (2); bapt/bur. Withern.
1724-1726	Lister Fitzwilliam	son of WF (3); bapt/bur. Withern.
1726-1777	Robert Vyner	of Gautby; Lincolnshire MP.
1777-1799	Robert Vyner (2)	son of RV (1); Gautby; Lincs MP.
1799-1810	Robert Vyner (3)	son of RV (2); Gautby; Lincs MP.
1810-1872	Robert Vyner (4)	son of RV (3); Gautby.
1872-1883	Henry FC Vyner	nephew of RV (4); Newby Hall.
1883-1915	Robert C de G Vyner	brother of HFCV; Newby Hall.
1915-1920	Lady M Compton-Vyner	dau of RCdeGV; Newby Hall.

Appendix VIII
Withern with Stain Parish Council Chairmen 1894-1976

1894-1907	The Revd FA Glover
1907-16	JT Marshall
1916-25	A Enderby
1925-42	C Burkitt
1946	J Elliott
1948-51	AE Frankum
1951-52	CD Pocklington
1952-54	JW Perkins
1955-62	AE Frankum
1962-64	JW Bullivant
1964-69	GW Barber
1969-73	FE Mountain
1973-76	Mrs C Vinter

Appendix IX
Population

	Withern	Stain	Tothill	Gayton	Strubby/ Woodthorpe	Aby
1086	250*		70*	220*	150*	
1563◆	n.a.	10~	70~	250~	n.a.	70~
1718‡	240~				150~	
1801	295		72	238	195	122
1831	390		67	306	201	
1861	528	[11]	61	331	295	407
1901	403		45	209	215	267
1931	334		39	155	187	240
1961	296		31	148	224	213

*	estimate based on Domesday Survey [Tothill may have included Gayton]
◆	Diocesan Return of Resident Families 1563 multiplied by 5
~	number of families multiplied by 5
‡	replies to Diocesan questionnaire by the Revd William Jones

Appendix X
Main Sources Used

Grimsby Reference Library [NE Lincs Lib. Services]:
Census Returns 1801-91
Kelly's, Pigot's and White's Directories of Lincolnshire

Lincolnshire Archives:
Alford Court of Sewers/8 Laws, etc [re Withern Eau]
Bishop's Correspondence
DBE 8 & 9 [Diocesan Board of Education papers]
Dioc Gibson VvV: 5/385
FL e 4 [Lists of Withern Rectors and Cantarists]
LD 85/5, 85/11 and 85/12 [Fitzwilliam/Stovin]
3 Nott/2 and Field 2/1 [Newcomen/Withern Mill]
Lindsey QS: Land Tax Assessments
Lindsey QS: Settlement Examinations
Misc Dep 74/1 & 2: Woodthorpe manor sale Arthur Hall to John Ballett, 1593
Misc Dep 165/4/1: letter from the Revd Wm Layng
Misc Dep 246/1: Withern Churchwardens' Accounts
Strubby Parish Registers and Terriers
Strubby Parish 13/3 Overseers' A/cs 1801-37
Sub 5/6/94
Tothill Parish Registers and Terriers
Withern Tithe Award, 1839
Withern Parish documents and National School Logbooks
Withern Parish Registers and Terriers
Wills, Inventories, Dissenters' Certificates, Presentations, etc.

London Metropolitan Archives:
Stovin Papers [Accession 1156]

National Monuments Record Centre, Swindon:
Details and photographs of Listed Buildings

West Yorkshire Archives Service, Leeds:
Newby Hall Collection [Ref NH 2355]: Lincolnshire estates of Robert Vyner
at Authorpe, Strubby, Withern, Mablethorpe & Theddlethorpe, 1754

Withern-with-Stain Parish Council:
Minute Books 1894-1976 and Enclosure Award 1840

Publications:
Bomber Command Losses 1939-40, WR Chorley
Bonney's Church Notes, Archdeacon Bonney, 1847
Calendar of State Papers 30 Henry 8, vol 1
Chancery Inq. PM Series II 204/157
Coastal Erosion in East Lincolnshire, AEB Owen, *The Lincolnshire
          Historian*, Spring 1952, No. 9
Domesday Book: Lincolnshire [gen. ed. John Morris], 1986
English Episcopal Acta 1 - Lincoln 1067-1185, ed David M Smith, 1980
History of Alford, the Revd RC Dudding

History of Lincolnshire, SLHA [various volumes]
History of Ormsby, WO Massingberd, 19th cent.
History of Saleby with Thoresthorpe, the Revd RC Dudding, 1922
History of the Vyner Family & The Vyner Pedigree, HW Vyner, 1885
Lincoln Diocese Documents 1450-1544, ed Andrew Clark, 1914
Lincolnshire Air War 1939-45, Book Two, S Finn, 1983
Lincolnshire Gleanings, Roy Fisk, c1985, quoting The Lincoln Date Book
Lincolnshire in the 17th and 18th Centuries, Charles Brears, 1940
Lincolnshire Notes & Queries
Lincolnshire Record Soc. volumes, especially 4, 23, 34, 72, 78, 85 & 87
Lincolnshire Wills 1500-1600, ed AR Maddison, 1881
Lincolnshire Windmills, Peter Dolman, 1986
Lincolnshire Windmills - Part I Post Mills, Rex Wailes, the Newcomen
        Society 1953, reprinted by Friends of Heckington Mill 1991
Notes on the History of Well, the Revd HR Tatham: LAAS Vol 30
Notices of Louth, 1834
Recollections of a Lincolnshire Miller, ed Gordon Willson, 1994
Scandinavian Settlement Names in the E Midlands, G Fellows Jensen, 1978
'Stamford Mercury' newspaper
The Book of the Lincolnshire Seaside, David Robinson, 1981
The Church Bells of Lincolnshire
The Compton Census of 1676, ed Anne Whiteman, 1986
The Diaries of George Langton 1647-1727, ed DH Hamilton, 1998
The Flight of the Mew Gull, Alex Henshaw, 1980 [reprint 1998]
The Lay Subsidy of 1334 for Lincolnshire, RE Glasscock: LAAS Vol 10 pt2
The Lincoln & Lincolnshire Cabinet .. for 1827, JW Drury, Lincoln, 1827
The 'Revolt of the Field' in Lincs, Rex C Russell, NUAW, 1956
The Water Drinkers in Lindsey 1837-60, Rex Russell, 1987
Victoria County History of Lincolnshire, Vol 2

Private Sources:
Colcroft House deeds
The Foresters' Heritage Trust
1592821 Sgt L McGowan's flight engineer's log book
The Rechabites Friendly Society, Manchester
Rex C Russell: notes
Stovin family: RH Stovin estate papers
Withern Cricket Club Score Books c1948-60
Withern & District Horticultural Society Minute Book 1901-17
Withern Methodist Church papers
Withern Mill: Grace Wright's Memories of her Childhood

SHORT GENERAL INDEX